MW01291728

Advanced Guitar Theory and Technique Applied to the Metal and Shred Genres

Copyright © 2012 by L. Herman

First Printing, 2012
Rev 1.2

ISBN-13: 978-1478387374

ISBN-10: 1478387378

### Advanced Guitar Theory and Technique Applied To the Metal and Shred Genres

*This book is written for the intermediate to advanced metal or shred guitarist. It will not teach you the names of the notes or how to hold a pick or how to play an open D chord, etc. This book assumes that you are already well on your way to becoming a good guitarist and feel the need to break through to the next level. This book will teach you the theory that is involved when writing and performing solos so that you are always able to play in tune with the backing chords. Modal theory is explained in a way that always keeps the metal and shred player in mind. Each lesson is explicitly written to serve the metal guitarist with usable examples and exercises that fit within the metal genre. This is not to say that modal theory can't be applied to any other style of music. Quite the contrary, you will come to understand modal theory and be able to apply it to any other genre of music that you wish.*

*You will also learn the other half of the metal guitar equation, techniques such as speed picking and the execution of arpeggios. These are two of the main staples that define shred guitar. In the picking section both alternate and economy picking are covered. The arpeggio section is intertwined with references to modal theory so that you will not only be able to execute the technique; you will actually be able to incorporate them into your own solos no matter what key you are playing in.*

*Throughout this book you will also receive tips and insights to aide you in your quest to become a better, more complete musician. Tips and insights ranging from how to get more out of your practice sessions to what problem areas to watch out for before you even attempt to learn a new technique. This book contains a wealth of knowledge that can be used as a reference for many years to come. It is my hope that you will enjoy studying its contents as much as I have enjoyed writing it.*

*L. Herman*

If you are like most guitarists, including myself, you will page through this book seeking out TAB and disregard much of the written word. This is an acceptable way to approach this book. Seek out parts that you like and want to learn about and give them a try. Work through the TAB that looks interesting and play it. But after this initial approach has begun to slow and you find yourself wanting more, go back and read. TAB can be a very useful tool when it comes to learning all aspects of guitar. But it can't completely explain certain concepts and insights. You will find that much of what is written will explain from multiple angles what you are playing, how to apply it, and problem areas to watch out for. You may also find some of it inspirational and Zen like. We can find TAB on any scale, mode, or song and it can only teach us so much. The "real teaching" is contained within the written words.

Enjoy!

*To enjoy practice as much as performance is the key to reaching our goals.*

# PRACTICE

Practice is obviously the key to becoming a better guitarist. Hopefully at the level of playing that you are at now, you enjoy practicing and it's not a chore. If it is a chore to you, I don't have a lot of advice for you. I've always enjoyed practicing. Even running scales up and down the neck I find enjoyable. I enjoy playing along with a metronome, learning music theory, and all of the things that many other guitarists find mundane. The bottom line is that I realize all of these things help to make me a better guitarist and getting better at our craft is very satisfying.

Now you will ask "What should I practice to get better?" or "What practice routine should I use?" The answer is; that depends on what you want to improve on and what you feel like getting better at on any given day. I don't use any strict practice routine but if that is what works for you that's great. How many hours a day should you practice? As many as you want and are able to. As long as you are having fun you will get so much more out of your practice sessions. I will give you a few tips on practicing that can really help you make great strides but it really all comes down to you having to want to practice and get better. If you don't have the drive to get better you will just stay at the level you are currently at, which isn't always a bad thing. Nobody has to learn a thousand different arpeggios and 100 scales to be great. You might be happy being at the level you are at now. But, if you want to get better and play this style of music, here are some essential practice tips to help you get the most out of your practice sessions.

# Pain!!

If you feel pain, **STOP!!** You should never feel pain. Serious injuries can and do occur. I couldn't imagine putting in years of practice only to get an injury that prohibits me from ever playing again. The guitar is too much a part of my life to allow this to happen. Many guitarists want to get better so bad and push themselves so hard that they believe learning the instrument is like lifting weights. No pain no gain! This is very, very wrong when practicing guitar. The truth is that if you feel pain, you are playing it wrong. Stop immediately and regroup. Do not jeopardize your playing career by being stubborn. And realize that, if it hurts, you are playing it wrong, and why would you practice playing something wrong? Do not jeopardize this part of your life.

# Make each and every note perfect

If you are learning a new lick, arpeggio, or anything for that matter, concentrate on playing each and every note cleanly. Don't fall into a rut by practicing a great lick but always missing a note somewhere in there or getting too much string noise or it just feels odd to play. Concentrate on the problem area and fix it! If you have a really cool 16 note run that is fun to play and sounds great but two notes out of the sixteen are tricky and you miss them half of the time, slow down and fix those two notes. Sometimes we, myself included, get into the mindset that two bad notes out of sixteen isn't bad at all, and we mentally decide that the lick is finished. It's not! Practice hitting those two notes!!

# Never practice mistakes

Many guitarists try to force a lick into submission. If they can't play a certain lick they will keep playing it over and over. This is actually a great trait to have, the drive to say "I'm going to get this lick down no matter how many times I have to play it." But if you keep playing it wrong, all you are doing is practicing how to play it wrong. We want to practice how to play it right. So slow it down, play it perfectly at a slow, even pace and build speed as you are able too. Mistakes should be avoided at all costs.

# Play relaxed

While you are practicing a new and difficult technique or lick have you ever noticed the other parts of your body other than your hands? Is your body all tense? Does your forearm get tired? Are you gritting your teeth? Do you tense up your shoulders and biceps? Relax! Breathe! We want our playing to flow effortlessly. What would happen if I told you to play your favorite lick that you are totally comfortable playing in any situation but I said now play it while flexing your bicep and keeping your shoulders very rigid? I will bet that you would not play it nearly as well as you normally do. I have taught beginners how to play a simple chord only to see them straining, trying to force their fingers to move to the proper frets. I always tell them to relax, calm down, don't fight it. You probably remember how hard it was for you to fret a simple open C chord when you were first learning. Now look at how effortless it is for you to hit that chord. Always try to keep your muscles relaxed and don't tense up while you practice.

# Own the lick

When you have a new lick down, do you really have it down? Can you play it at any tempo? Can you alter the dynamics of it by palm muting or digging your pick in harder? Can you play it in other positions and string groups? Can you play it in reverse? Can you add vibrato to any of the notes? When we learn new licks and techniques we want to integrate them fully into our playing. Learning a new lick in only one position and only at a certain tempo is far from being fully integrated into our mental library. We need to be able to use this lick at multiple tempos, multiple keys and positions, and multiple styles like legato, picking, palm muting, adding pinch harmonics on certain notes, etc. When you can alter a lick in any way you wish to, then you own it. So don't call a lick finished and stop practicing it when you are so close to being able to utilize it in different ways. Just a little more time really playing the lick opens up so many possibilities. This is the way that better guitarists seem to never run out of licks. They know how to apply favorite, stock licks that they possess in their arsenal to many different situations, musical styles, keys, tempos, etc…

This is also what defines your particular style. You took that lick and started it with palm muting followed by a nice legato section and finished it off with a whole step bend with a perfectly in time wicked wide vibrato! Now it's your lick. You own it! So practice playing it in reverse. Change the tempo. Play it in another key. You will soon find that that one lick will turn into its own entity and that you can summon and use it in any situation, key, style, or genre.

# Natural Talent

## How do you get to Carnegie Hall??     Natural Talent     (*I don't think so*)

When it comes to guitar ***I don't believe there is such a thing as natural talent***. Sure some guitarists pick it up quicker than others but your natural talent will only get you so far. A good work ethic and the will to get better will beat out natural talent every single time. I believe the only natural talent in music is note choice and style. With enough practice you can perform any lick known to mankind. The natural talent part comes from the music that is in your head. I hear some of my favorite guitarists play a solo and I just think wow! I never would have thought to play that arpeggio over that chord, or that note to end the solo, or that phrasing. I could play the exact same solo as them after they wrote it. I can normally learn just about any solo save but a few. But the real talent came when they wrote it.

So if you don't think you can be as good as you want to be because you don't have enough "natural talent", let me stop you right there. You think Yngwie just picked up a guitar one day and played like that? He just knew music theory? Steve Vai never practiced, yet he is still able to play the way he does? Most great guitarists never put their instrument down. They practiced because they loved playing.

Let me put it another way. Let's say there is a tough lick that you just believe to be impossible because you don't have enough "natural talent". So you don't even try to play it. If I offered you $1,000,000 in cash if you can play that lick in two weeks would you be able to play it? I would imagine you would have that lick nailed in one weeks' time easily, natural talent or not.

Now a seven foot tall basketball player has natural talent. A pitcher that can throw 98 mph, a football player that is 6'8" 325lbs, and a sprinter that can run… I don't know, really, really fast, all have natural talent. We as guitarists rely on practice.

I remember when I attended college and I witnessed all of the students who skated through high school barely cracking a book. They always seemed so much smarter than I was and they most likely were. We took the same 100 level courses and they breezed through them while I had to study. We received the same grades but I had to work for them. Then we got to the 200 level courses and I still had to study. They saw their grades slip and blamed it on bad teaching but still passed. Then when we got to the 300 level courses I started seeing them dropping out at an increased rate. The school is not fair and full of bad teachers was their most common reason. I still studied hard but not any harder than I did with the 100 level courses. They just never learned how to study, or didn't want to study. It always seemed like such a waste of "natural talent" to me. So, hard work beat out natural talent.

## Learn How to Learn

When we are learning anything, especially guitar techniques and theory, every one learns differently. How do **YOU** learn new material best? Do you slowly and methodically learn each part until you have it down? Not moving on to the next part until you have mastered the previous part. Do you just blaze through it and come back later to fix the problem areas? Do you learn the difficult part first or the easy part? Do you have to understand the theory behind a lick before you attempt to play it? Do you play it over and over for hours or do you play it for five minutes and then come back to it the next day? Or in an hour? There is no right or wrong answer here.

My point is that you need to figure out how **YOU** learn new techniques and theory in the most efficient way possible. Pay attention to how **YOU** are best able to learn. And realize that this can change over time and also depend on the technique or lesson that you are practicing. My only advice to you is to practice what you feel like practicing on that day. When you do this practice is enjoyable and you actually want to do it, thus increasing the benefits that you receive from the practice session.

I have sat for hours trying to learn a certain lick or technique. I have also spent about five minutes practicing something only to abandon it and come back to it at a later date. It felt like work to me. And I know that, at least in my case, if it feels like work, then I'm not getting much out of my practice session. I believe one hour of intense practice where you are paying attention and giving 100% to learning is probably equal to ten hours of messing around or jamming. I don't have any specific warm up routine or a set of licks that I practice every day. But, I am honest with myself and if I have neglected a certain aspect of my playing for a week or two I make sure to go back and reinforce it. So strive to *learn how to learn* and remember that no two guitarists are identical in this aspect.

## Play In Front of Other People

This may seem obvious because it is most likely what we are trying to accomplish as musicians. Playing in front of other people teaches us how to overcome stage fright and how to cover up mistakes. And trust me, you will make mistakes! If you aren't making any mistakes then you are not playing difficult music and you aren't challenging yourself. Learn how to salvage a solo after you messed up the beginning. The majority of the time the audience won't even notice. Other times if you successfully salvage the solo they will think that you added your own little lick or style to it. Either way, they think that you are playing exactly what you mean to be playing.

Playing in front of other people also teaches us how to be better performers, which can be difficult playing the kind of music that we do. It wouldn't be much fun to go see Metallica play only to have the lights dim and the curtains open and they are all sitting on stools, motionless. They might play flawlessly but I doubt that they would sell out many more concerts if that was their new style. So when you play in front of people, even just a friend or two, remember that this is a good time to practice performing.

# Learn at least some music theory

I believe I made more progress after I started to learn theory than at any other time in my years of playing. You don't need to learn every scale in the book or the name of every chord ever created. Although, that would be great if you did! One of the best things about learning at least some musical theory is that you begin to see the fretboard in a different way. Everything starts to make more sense. You will see patterns and shapes on the fretboard and be able to jump to them at will. It won't matter to you what key the song is in. If you want to play a happy solo you will know what to do. Bluesy, classical, eerie, it won't matter. It really frees up your playing. The other big advantage is, even if you're playing covers and not writing your own solos, you see the shapes on your fretboard. You don't have to think of the frets as numbers anymore. "This part of the solo is on the $12^{th}$, $14^{th}$, and $15^{th}$ frets". You will be thinking "I'm in E minor, and I can use any of these notes within the E minor scale and I will be in tune". Even if you get lost onstage and start to butcher your solo, you can save it by at least playing in tune. If you know what key you are in and how to apply a little music theory, you will be able to play in tune. Solo saved!!

Learning theory is not as difficult as it seems. The difficult part, as I will let you know shortly, is that you must learn seven different patterns. Yes, there is some memorizing involved. No, I do not have an easy way to do this. Time and effort is all that is required. And, it's not like learning seven patterns is all that difficult. You probably know how to play ten different songs already and these took you months to master.

Just learn these seven patterns and you will be 75% of the way to learning music theory. Trust me! If you just spend some time learning all seven patterns you will open up yo ur playing tremendously. There is no way to learn theory if you do not learn the seven patterns. No short cuts. No alternate methods. Just spend some time and learn the patterns. It's all downhill from there.

# Identifying and Isolating the Problem

This is an art all in itself. This is also perhaps one of the most important lessons you can ever learn. When you are learning a new technique or lick, particularly a longer one, and are struggling to get it down, what part of it *exactly* is holding you back? If it's a sixteen note run and you always mess up in the middle of it, what is the problem? Is it the part where you switch to a different string? Is it your picking hand that is the problem? Is it a synchronization problem? Is your fret hand not precise enough and you are getting string noise? Or do you not have the lick engrained enough in your head and fingers so that you are able to play the notes without even thinking about them? Normally, it's only one minor problem holding you back. Don't keep playing the run and messing up in the middle of it. Work on just that one small problematic part because you have the rest of the lick down pretty well and don't need to spend as much time on it as you do with the problem area.

You must also be honest about hearing your own playing. You can't work on a problem area if you don't realize that it's a problem for you. As we advance as guitarists we can actually "feel" mistakes. We can "feel" when we didn't fret a note properly in our hand. We can "feel" in our picking hand if our pick angle got a little out of whack. We can "feel" our fingers struggle to hit a note when we don't have a lick mastered yet.

Whenever you experience any of these symptoms ask yourself why. Find out the part of the lick that caused these symptoms. It is probably only one little minute part. And once you diagnose the problem fix it! Now once it is fixed the next time you learn a new lick that has a similar pattern or technique you will learn it that much quicker. Spending time on your problem areas helps you to master the instrument at a much faster pace than you would be able to by just blindly practicing for hours.

# What Tone To Use When Practicing

This is a tricky subject and I firmly believe that there are no rules. My personal belief is that you can have two different answers to this question. A big part of learning to play guitar, especially of the metal genre, is learning how to control the instrument. Awesome, distorted, heavy metal, high gain guitar in a live setting can be difficult to control. Feedback and loud string noise can be difficult to tame. This would lead you to believe that the best tone to use during practice would be this sort of high gain, distorted type. The other way of thinking is that when your guitar tone is that distorted, compressed, and let's throw a little bit of reverb or delay in there so we can get a nice thick tone, you can't hear the little nuances of your playing. You can't hear the part where you are not playing the lick as well as you could be because the distortion is masking your mistake. I guess I prefer to try to get my tone somewhere in the middle.

My practice tone is far from being brutally distorted. Yet, it's not even being close to being clean. It's a tone where I have to work to make it sound the way I want it to. I have to pick harder and cleaner to make it sound heavier. And, I have to lighten up and use different muting techniques to make it more mellow or clean.

The important thing to get across here is that you need to practice with both tones. You need to be able to control your instrument and be able to play in very loud situations where string noise and feedback can be a major issue. But, if you want to really advance in your playing, you also must be able to hear every little nuance of what you are playing. You have to be able to hear when you are playing a certain note or section sloppy. So in a nutshell, do whatever works for you. Try to find an in-between tone or tradeoff between a dirty and clean tone. Either way, come to the realization that both are important and you need to practice with both tones in order to be able to play some great, sick licks while at the same time keeping feedback and extra noise at bay.

# Warming Up

I personally do not have any specific warm up routine that I perform before I practice. Although I don't just pick up the guitar and start doing wide stretch string skipping licks either. When I pick up the guitar I just practice what I feel like practicing. And being that I normally start out practicing licks slowly, I naturally get my fingers warmed up during this time.

But, when playing live, many times you will not have the luxury to warm up at all. In these situations you should have a little warm up routine to get your fingers into playing shape quickly. I like to just perform trills on each finger. If you just trill a note as fast and as evenly as possible for 30 seconds on each finger (2$^{nd}$, 3$^{rd}$, 4$^{th}$) you can have your fret hand *fairly* warmed up in 90 seconds. When I say "fairly" warmed up I mean warmed up enough to make it through the first song without too much trouble. If I had my choice I would play for 45 minutes before I go on stage and be totally warmed up but this is seldom the case.

## Don't Forget To Warm Up Your Picking Hand

When you warm up don't fail to include your picking hand. Many times it takes longer for our picking hand to warm up than it does our fretting hand. I try to play one of the speed picking practice licks that you will see later in the book for 30 seconds or so. These can also warm your fret hand up as well. I then run through a few arpeggios for 30 seconds.

So if we follow this routine including the fret hand warm up routine we can be at least warmed up enough to play a song in 90s + 30s+ 30s = 150s   (2 ½ minutes).

# Finger Strength

I have never understood the need for finger strength when it comes to playing guitar. I have seen finger exercise contraptions being sold to guitarists and have never understood the need for them. I believe we as guitarists don't need more "strength" in our fingers, we need more "precision".

How much "strength" does it really take to push a very thin metal wire down a millimeter or two anyways? There are many bodybuilders that have a grip that could most likely crush my hand during a handshake but does that make them more predisposed to being a better guitarist? I don't believe so. I think that when we are learning a new lick or technique, we too many times struggle so hard to play it and try to force our fingers to do what we are telling them to do that our hand gets tired. This has nothing to do with strength. This is where the precision part comes to play.

When you fret a note properly it takes so little pressure to hold the string against the fretboard that it is almost not worth worrying about. If we wanted to compare the musculature of our hands to real world examples we would want them to be sprinters or long distance runners as opposed to a body builder that can squat 500 pounds. We don't need more strength in our fingers. We need **precision, agility** and **stamina.** We should strive to fret every note very precisely while being able to quickly move to different frets and positions. What we don't need is to try to "muscle" our fingers and force them into arriving at the destination of our choice.

Also, when you have your hand in the proper position with the thumb behind the fretboard you get much better leverage and are able to fret the notes much easier. So strive for more accuracy, not strength.

# Guitar and Typing

Yes that is a strange heading. This is about how we memorize licks. When we are first starting out we are thinking of each individual note and fret number and this way of thinking greatly diminishes how fast we are able to play a lick and how easily we are able to move it around and play it in different positions. We need to think of the lick as its own entity that we can play without thinking.

I cannot type very well but I am able to get by. I know many, many people who amaze me that they can type so fast. I have witnessed people of different genders, ages, and body types able to type whatever I am saying to them verbatim without even glancing at the keyboard. So my question is, how is this so different from playing guitar? They are moving their fingers to very specific spots, very accurately, without looking at their fingers to help aide them. Isn't that what we are striving to do as guitarists? So literally millions of people are able to do what we wish to do yet we have to work so hard and practice at it? Many times someone who can type asks me how I am able to hit all of those notes and remember where to put my fingers at such a high rate of speed. But are my fingers moving any faster than theirs are when they are typing? No they are not.

If a typist can learn how to move their fingers in much the same way that we desire to, then surely this can't be that difficult to achieve. And if you already know how to type then you should know exactly what I am talking about.

## Think of Licks as Words

When people type on a keyboard, they normally don't think about the actual letters that they are typing. If you ask them to type their name they just go click, click, click…..done. They aren't "spelling" their name; they have just done it so many times that their fingers move in a certain pattern that is equal to their name. Also, while they are typing their name they are not even thinking about it. They are already looking at or thinking about the next word that they are going to type. This is what we want to be able to do when we play a lick. We want to have it be so ingrained in our fingers that while we are playing it we are already thinking about where we are next going to go.

Think about when you sign your name. Are you "spelling" your name? Think about how fast you can sign your name without even thinking about it. Can you be talking to someone while you are signing your name? Do you ever even think about signing your name or are you already thinking about what you are going to do next?

## The Power of Repetition

You have signed your name so many times that you don't need to think about it and your hand just performs the motion. You can sign your own name at lightning speeds. But let's try this just to prove my point. Sign your name but use all capital letters. Try it and compare the two speeds. Or how about sign your name but purposely leave out any two letters. Your speed is suddenly gone and you are all of a sudden concentrating on how to "spell" your name. This is why we practice playing repetitive licks, so that they can become just a motion to us. We don't think about the lick or the notes that we are playing. We have practiced it so many times that our fingers just perform the motion and while they are doing their job this allows us to use our minds to think about what we are going to do next.

# Keep a Practice Log

You don't need to keep track of everything that you have practiced or make a schedule, but keeping a dedicated notebook by our side can be a great asset to us. How many times have you said to yourself "How did that lick go that I was working on"? Or maybe "What was that cool pattern that I saw"? When you have a notebook by your side when you are practicing you should just jot down the basic idea you had or just a very basic TAB diagram.

Why would we practice for two hours straight and discover a cool lick, technique, idea, riff, song, lyric, tone, fingering, etc only to forget it the very next day? A note book and a pencil that costs us a whopping $2 could solve this problem. Heck, just write all over this book. Make little notes to yourself. Don't spend your time trying to remember something that you thought was important. If you feel that it is important make a little note.

So when you practice just have a regular notebook by you to jot down ideas and such. Once I started doing this I was shocked at how quickly it filled up. I wouldn't write in it every day or every practice session. I would just jot things down occasionally when I felt it was necessary. It can be a great way to help discipline yourself without putting in any effort.

Occasionally I go back and look through the pages of notebooks I have kept by my side during practice. I see that I had some great and some not so great ideas. I see licks and exercises that I have long since forgotten. However, even with the forgotten exercises I pick them up very, very quickly because I have a reference that I have written for myself. Nobody else needs to understand what I recorded in the note book but I do. And it has been a huge help to me.

# Synchronization Is the Key

We need to have both of our hands work in concert with each other in order to play quickly, effortlessly, and accurately. Imagine everything that has to happen in order for us to play. Our head tells our body to play a lick. Then both of our hands magically perform two completely different actions while in our heads we are thinking about what we are going to play next. It really is amazing if you think about it. And it all comes from "muscle memory".

To play accurately, effortlessly, and quickly requires us to concentrate on both of our hands during practice. We can't just stare at our fret hand when learning a new lick or technique. We need to concentrate on each of them. Many guitarists work only on their fret hand which is very limiting and will not cure what ails our technique. Think about it. Either hand can throw a monkey wrench into our riff at any time. Both hands require very separate and different practice exercises to help emphasize the technique we are trying to master. If we wanted to run faster would we only focus on our right leg and ignore the left? Will a boxer only throw a right hook and not a left? Not a good one.

The most difficult part of learning a new lick or technique is getting our hands to work together and not against each other. Perhaps we are further along with our fret hand so we try to "rush" our picking hand to catch up. You can always feel this when practicing, the feeling that something is not right and feels "funny" when we play it.

This is why we must practice slowly at times, so that we can isolate and define first, the hand that is giving us the problem and second the actual movement that we are struggling with. Don't struggle with a lick and keep staring at your fret hand when the problem may very likely be with your picking hand. Always think of your two hands as one tool that performs whatever we wish it to.

# Dexterity Exercises

I'm not a huge fan of practicing chromatic exercises very often but they do definitely have their uses for certain aspects of our playing. Here is a great exercise that helps us keep our fret hand fingers low to the fretboard thus assisting us in achieving greater speeds because our fingers don't have to travel as great a distance. It can be quite a finger twister so just concentrate on playing it accurately and don't worry about speed.

With this exercise **keep your fingers down on the frets** and only move the finger that you need to fret the next note. So we are only moving one finger at a time. This is much more difficult than it seems.

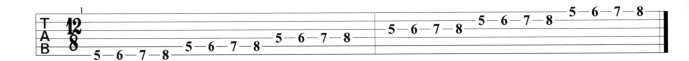

## The word "Chromatic" means that we are not using any scale and are able to play any note on the fretboard.

And as always, let's not forget the inverse of this exercise. With this one when you release a finger to allow you to play the lower note instead of just lifting it, put it on the next fret where it will used. This lick starts with our 4th finger. For the next note move the 4th finger to the B string 5th fret and leave it there while you strike the 4th fret on the high E string. Next note move your 3rd finger to the B string 4th fret and leave it until needed while you strike the 3rd fret on the high E string. This exercise helps us to move our fingers to where they will soon be needed.

**Again, we are only moving one finger at a time and the others stay on the fretboard.**

**The word "Diatonic" means that we are playing within a scale or mode.**

**We would use ONLY the notes that are contained within a scale.**

Mostly, chromatic exercises help us to get our brains and hands in synch with each other and encourage finger independence. Some guitarists use them often. I recommend using them rather sparingly, but there are no rules and if you get a great benefit from them, then by all means, practice them often.

The reason that I don't use them very often is because I have always felt "Why would I practice putting my fingers in places that I am not going to actually use in my own playing"? It's extremely rare, *if ever*, that I would use the chromatic scale in my soloing. So I just came to the belief that if I am going to practice an exercise why *wouldn't* I do it "diatonically"?

**I will give you a couple more chromatic exercises but after this page every exercise will be "diatonic" to a scale.**

Both of these next two exercises are brain and finger twisters.

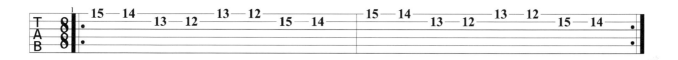

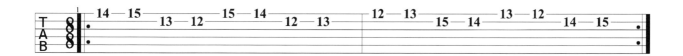

It's easy to make up our own chromatic exercises. We don't have to worry about scales or where to put our fingers. Just make up your own patterns that are difficult to play and practice them slowly and deliberately.

# Legato Exercises

Legato exercises are extremely useful to us. It's great to play around with some chromatic exercises once in a while but **legato exercises build speed, stamina, precision, dexterity, and help us to visualize the fretboard**. For these exercises I have just randomly chosen fret locations and positions but you should move these around to different spots and try different patterns and fingerings. Practice them on all strings as well. Let's start with a few basic ones.

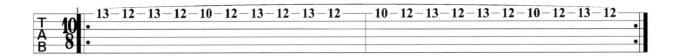

The above exercise really helps work on our pinky and is very usable in our solos.

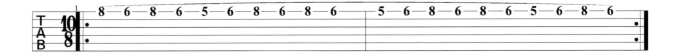

This is the same pattern but uses different fingers and gives us a bit more stretch.

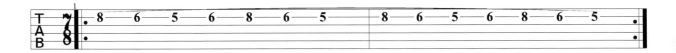

This is a pattern we use often in many solos.

With all of these exercises notice that we only pick the first note and that's it. See if you can play these for 30 seconds straight without using your picking hand at all. Strive for a nice even volume and tempo.

Now let's begin to add more strings and positions into our legato exercises.

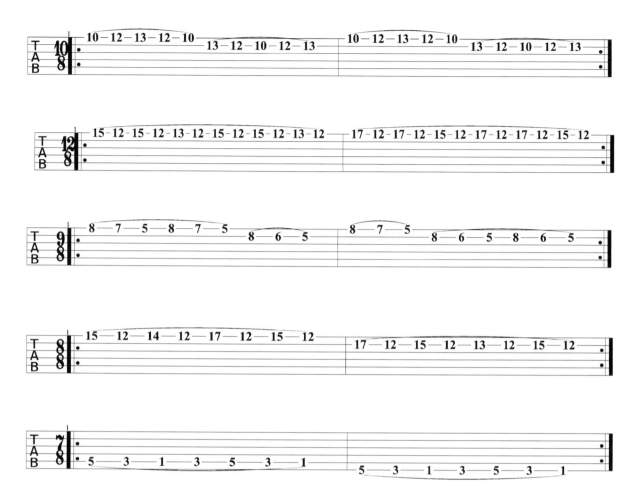

It can be tricky when working on the lower two strings with a wider stretch but it can really give you a great workout. Make sure to **STOP** if it hurts though.

And finally, let's work on a very useful, long run that crosses all of the strings and sounds great when we play it. You can pick each note when you start a new string but try and see if you can play this without using your picking hand at all.

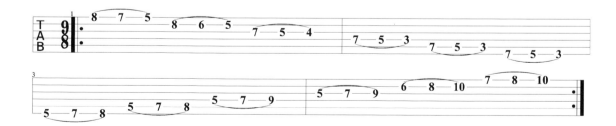

# MODAL THEORY

Learning music theory can be an intimidating endeavor. I will try to explain modal theory in a way that will not only be easier to understand but also extremely useful in your playing. Using modal theory will allow you to play in tune against nearly any chord or key. Don't be intimidated by all of the terminology. It really is much easier than it sounds. Many guitarists start by learning the pentatonic box or boxes. I started this way as well but found that when advancing to modal scales, the pentatonic boxes didn't help me at all and actually confused me.

So let's get started with the very basic. There are 7 notes in a scale. Yes, I know there are scales that have 8 and scales that have 5 and so forth but all of those other scales are actually made by adding or subtracting notes from the scale we will be concentrating on. The scale we will be learning is the base of all other scales; **The Major scale**. Once we learn this we can use all of its modes and play a solo in any style that we choose.

Let's look at a few "shapes". There are only three shapes contained within the major scale. Fingering wise you could call them 1 3 4, 1 2 4, and 1 3 4 (stretch).

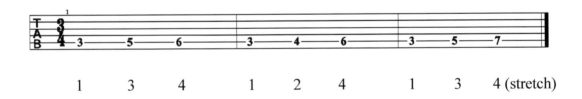

1      3      4       1      2      4       1      3      4 (stretch)

The entire major scale is made up of only these three shapes. That's easy enough right? Remember, we don't want to think about what fret we are on. We only want to think about shapes. This way, we can move these "shapes" around anywhere on the fretboard without thinking. Now with these three shapes we will learn to apply them into seven different patterns. Seven patterns because that is how many notes are in the scale.

Let's look at these shapes in a more visual way. Let's look at them on the fretboard. The actual fret doesn't matter to us because we are only trying to remember the shapes.

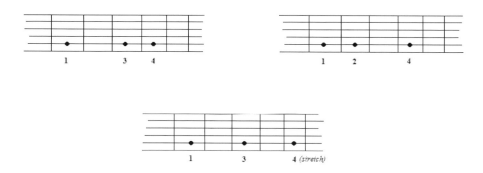

With these three shapes we can play a vast variety of scales and modes.

Now in the next section of the book we will start learning music theory, Modal Theory in particular. To learn this you must put in a little bit of effort. ***There is no way that you can learn music theory without learning a few patterns!*** *Seven to be exact.* You need to practice these patterns until they become second nature to you.

Now when learning these patterns you not only have to learn them. You have to be able to p*lay* them in order. The order that they go in is just as important as actually learning the patterns. So, in a nut shell:

***Learn the seven patterns!!***

***Be able to play them in order!!***

***Know the name of the pattern!!***

***The names of the modes in order are:***

| **Aeolian** | **Locrian** | **Ionian** | **Dorian** | **Phrygian** | **Lydian** | **Mixolydian** |
|:---:|:---:|:---:|:---:|:---:|:---:|:---:|
| At | Larry's | I | Do | Play | Lydian | Music |

# You Must Bite the Bullet and Learn These 7 Patterns!!

## It is not possible to learn music theory without learning these patterns!!

## This is the most difficult part of learning music theory!

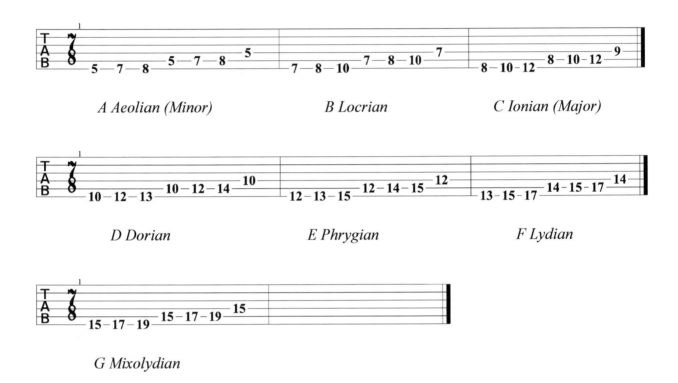

*A Aeolian (Minor)*          *B Locrian*          *C Ionian (Major)*

*D Dorian*          *E Phrygian*          *F Lydian*

*G Mixolydian*

These particular patterns are in the key of A minor which is very common in shred and metal music. Don't worry about understanding this right now; I will explain it later in the book. Also, try to remember the names of each pattern as you play them. It may not seem important now but later in the book you will see how important it is.

## Now Practice These Patterns Until You Can Play Them All Effortlessly!!

## I started us out learning in the key of A minor for two reasons.

1. *These notes work very well in many metal songs.*
2. *This gives you a great way to remember the names of the notes.*

There are no sharps or flats in here. A Aeolian has the notes ABCDEFG. B Locrian has the notes BCDEFGA; C Ionian has the notes CDEFGAB; D Dorian has the notes DEFGABC and so on. I will explain this in more detail later in the chapter. So as you play these patterns you can learn the names of the notes as well. Being that there are no sharps or flats in this particular key you can even say the notes out loud as you are playing them.

The A minor scale is very popular in the metal genre. If you only learned this one scale in this one key you could be able to play solos in tune to quite a few metal songs. This scale will work over many (but not all) songs that are in the key of either A or E. And in our metal genre of music these are two of the most common keys that we will be playing in; the most common keys because they allow us to exploit the open E and A string.

In the next two pages you will learn the "full" seven patterns as they span across all six strings. **It is crucial that you learn these seven patterns**. They are just a continuation of the seven patterns that you just saw. If you want to learn any music theory, then you have to learn these. If you remember any lesson contained within these pages please know the importance of these seven patterns. With these 7 patterns you will begin to unlock and understand the power that modal theory can bestow upon you. Modal theory will allow you to understand the notes that you play. It will guide you and assist you in your choices while writing your own music. It will give you the ability to solo over any backing chords and be in tune. And it all begins with these seven patterns that take a minimal amount of work and practice while giving us a maximum amount of options and clarity.

Now that we have those seven note patterns that we learned previously down lets extend them so that we can play them across all of the strings. These are the exact same notes as we just learned but we are extending them so that we can use all of the strings.

# Again, Bite the Bullet and Learn These Patterns!!

**This is the last time I will ask you to memorize anything!!**
*(I promise)*

*Learn to play them legato. Learn to play them picking.*
*Learn to play them ascending. Learn to play then descending.*
*Get to know these seven patterns so well that you can play them in your sleep.*
*And, as before, try to remember the name of the pattern that you are playing!*

# Learning 3 or 4 of the patterns won't work!

# You MUST learn all 7 of them!

For now you can learn these patterns as I have written them. We will worry about moving them around to different keys later. But always try to remember that these are just patterns. Try not to think of which fret you are on. Concentrate only on the pattern that you are playing.

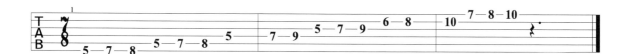

*A Aeolian (Minor)*

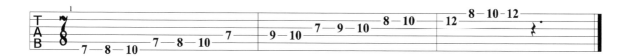

*B Locrian*

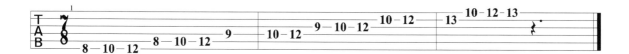

*C Ionian (Major)*

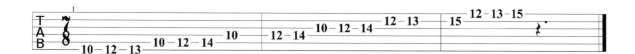

*D Dorian*

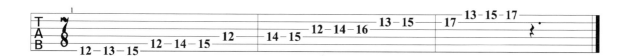

*E Phrygian*

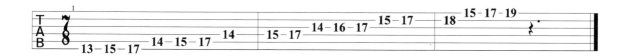

*F Lydian*

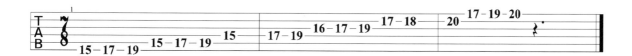

*G Mixolydian*

It is important to realize that, when learning these patterns, we are not really learning seven different scales. This is actually only one scale. We are just starting it out on each of the seven notes contained within the A minor scale.

| | |
|---|---|
| **Aeolian** mode contained the notes: | A  B  C  D  E  F  G |
| **Locrian** mode contained the notes: | B  C  D  E  F  G  A |
| **Ionian** mode contained the notes: | C  D  E  F  G  A  B |
| **Dorian** mode contained the notes: | D  E  F  G  A  B  C |
| **Phrygian** mode contained the notes: | E  F  G  A  B  C  D |
| **Lydian** mode contained the notes: | F  G  A  B  C  D  E |
| **Mixolydian** mode contained the notes: | G  A  B  C  D  E  F |

So as you can see, they all contain the same notes. We are just starting them out on the next note within the scale.

*A Aeolian / minor*

| | | | | | | | | | | | | | | |
|---|---|---|---|---|---|---|---|---|---|---|---|---|---|---|
| **A Aeolian** | A | B | C | D | E | F | G | A | B | C | D | E | F | G | A | B |
| **B Locrian** | | B | C | D | E | F | G | A | B | C | D | E | F | G | A | B |
| **C Ionian** | | | C | D | E | F | G | A | B | C | D | E | F | G | A | B |
| **D Dorian** | | | | D | E | F | G | A | B | C | D | E | F | G | A | B |
| **E Phrygian** | | | | | E | F | G | A | B | C | D | E | F | G | A | B |
| **F Lydian** | | | | | | F | G | A | B | C | D | E | F | G | A | B |
| **G Mixolydian** | | | | | | | G | A | B | C | D | E | F | G | A | B |

# About The Names

As I mentioned before, it is also important to learn these in order. I gave you a way to remember them but you can make up your own as well. Let's look at it again.

| MEMORY | MODE |
|--------|------|
| At | Aeolian / Minor |
| Larry's | Lydian |
| I | Ionian / Major |
| Do | Dorian |
| Play | Phrygian |
| Lydian | Lydian |
| Music | Mixolydian |

**And after this we repeat it. So Aeolian follows Mixolydian.**

*Conventional music theory always starts out, not in the Aeolian mode but in the Ionian mode. That is actually the "proper" way to think of it, but when I learned theory I based everything off of the Minor / Aeolian mode. My thinking was that I play the Aeolian mode much more than I ever play the Ionian mode.*

*The other reason was that since A minor has no sharps or flats, it would assist me in being able to know where any note is located anywhere on the fretboard. Quite honestly it doesn't really matter which mode you count as first as long as you know them in order.*

*Conventional music terminology bases everything off of the major scale and so it is always counted as the first scale. All of the rules still apply and you still come to the same result using my method. I just look at it a different way and I realize that my view is a little unorthodox compared to everyone else's. You can just as easily think of the Major / Ionian mode as the first mode and all of these lessons will still apply. At the end of this book I go into this concept in more detail if you want to understand why.*

***The important thing is to memorize, visualize, hear, understand, and play, automatically, each and every one of the seven patterns and names in order!***

## A Few Ways to Practice This Scale

There are many ways to practice this scale and ultimately you should do whatever works best for you. Practice it in multiple ways to help reinforce it. I'm also a firm believer in making the most out of our practice time so why don't we kill two birds with one stone and write some cool sounding licks that we can use in our own playing *and* use these to practice our scales at the same time.

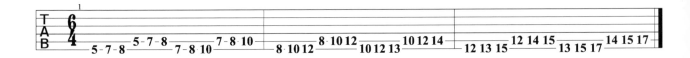

Practicing the scale on any two string sets helps you to visualize the fretboard in a more linear way. And let's not forget to use other string pairs as well.

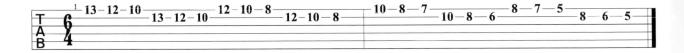

The above exercise is a good one because we are working with the B string which is tuned differently than the other strings. Notice how we use the same pattern but we have to shift it up one fret when we get to the B string.

And, let's not forget to play it in reverse as well.

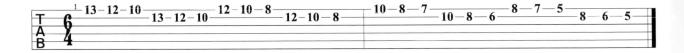

Here is a long run that is used often in quick metal runs.

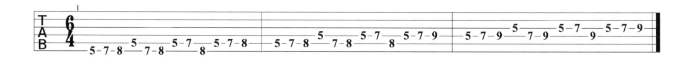

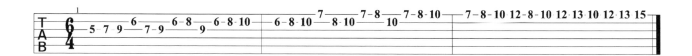

This next one works great for practicing legato or you can pick it which is great for practicing both economy picking and strict alternate picking.

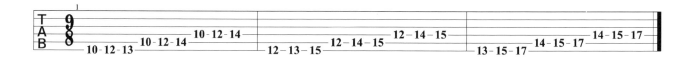

Here is another one that sounds cool and is usable in your soloing.

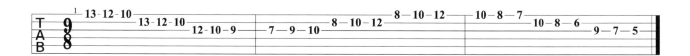

This one also should be played using both legato and picking techniques.

**Now make up some of your own and try to use them on all strings in all positions!**

# Beginning to Use and Understand What We Have Learned

Now that we have these patterns down let's start to learn a little theory. Notice that the Aeolian pattern that we learned starts on A. This tells us that we are playing A Aeolian. Aeolian is also called Minor so we can say we are playing in A minor.

### Now play any of the notes from the A minor scale over an A chord.

We are playing in tune and we get that nice *Minor* sort of sad sound when playing against an A chord. This mode is very popular in Metal music and there are quite a few guitarists who rely on this mode exclusively.

### Now try playing the same notes over a B chord.

Since we are playing over a B chord we would call this mode B Locrian. Why do we have a different name for the scale when we are playing the exact same notes as we did when we called it A minor? We certainly could still call it A minor but that can get confusing. Since we are playing over a B chord we will call it B Locrian. Locrian mode is not used too often in our metal genre. It has a sort of jazz type of sound to it.

### Now play the same notes over a C chord.

Hopefully you can begin to guess what we will call the scale now. We are playing C Ionian. Ionian is also called Major so we can call the scale C Major as well. Even though we are playing the exact same notes as the first time we tried this, now the notes sound happy against a C chord. Ionian mode is used a lot in country music and has a bright, uplifting sort of tone.

### Now we will play the same notes over a D chord.

And you guessed it. We will call this D Dorian. Dorian has a nice bluesy kind of tone and can be used in our metal genre.

## Now we will play the same notes over an E chord.

We are now playing E Phrygian. Phrygian mode is used a lot in metal music. This is definitely one of my favorites. It gets that nice evil, snake charmer kind of tone. And since so many songs in metal are in the key of E we can use this mode right away in a lot of our playing. This is one of the main reasons that I had us start out by learning these patterns in the key of A. This is because this key allows us to take advantage of the open E and A strings. And if you have played any metal songs before, you know how common it is to ride either of those two strings in a riff.

## Now try an F chord.

We are now playing F Lydian. Lydian mode has a distinct flavor to it that is hard to define. If you like Satriani, he uses this mode quite a bit.

## And finally we play the same notes over a G chord.

And we are now playing G Mixolydian. Mixolydian is not used very often in metal music.

Now to recap, we played the exact same notes that we had previously learned, which is actually only one scale. But, because we changed the chord that we were playing over, we took that one scale and gave it seven different names. Each of these names had a different flavor and we could hear how they sounded different as we changed the backing chord even though we never changed the actual notes that we were playing. So we took that one scale and without having to do much at all, we multiplied it into seven different scales that we can use as we choose.

Now in all reality, you most likely won't use all seven modes because they sound so different. You will probably rely on Aeolian and Phrygian a lot and maybe throw in a Dorian or Lydian mode on occasion. However, we now have the capability to play all seven modes and use them as we see fit.

# How to Use These Modes in Different Keys

Thus far we have only played these patterns in one key. Now we can move them around to give us almost unlimited possibilities with our soloing.

Let's start out with the Aeolian mode that we use quite often and are familiar with.

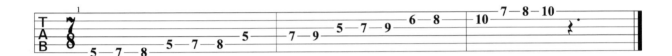

*A Aeolian (Minor)*

So we know that we can play this over an A chord and we like the way the notes sound against it. But let's say we are playing against an E chord and we want to get the same type of sound that we did when we were playing over the A chord. That's easy to do. We will just slide the whole pattern up so that it starts on an E. So let's move the whole pattern up to the 12$^{th}$ fret. Now we have:

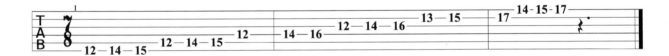

*E Aeolian (Minor)*

Notice that the patterns of these two scales are the exact same. We just started them in different spots. We started the pattern on an E instead of an A. This is why we want to think of these patterns as shapes as opposed to trying to remember what frets we are playing on. This way we don't really have very much to remember at all. Only our seven patterns need to be retained in our heads.

Let's try another one so we can be sure that we understand it. We know we like the E Phrygian modes tone when played in the key of E. It sounds dark, eerie, and evil. But now we want to play it in the key of G. We still want to get that same tone as we had when playing in E. We know that the E Phrygian mode looks like this:

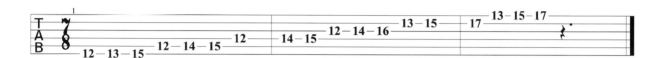

*E Phrygian*

So all we have to do is play this exact same pattern but start it out on a G. Let's start it out on the 3<sup>rd</sup> fret of the low E string. Remember, we play the exact same pattern. It will look like this:

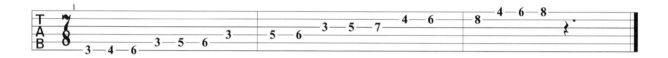

*G Phrygian*

Now see how easy this is? All we had to do was actually remember those seven **patterns**, and by doing that we increased the amount of scales at our disposal one thousand times over. We just take those seven patterns and move them to where we choose and we are in a different scale. Actually we are in a different **"mode"** of the same scale. This is where the term modal theory comes from.

## Looking at What We Have Learned From A Different Angle.

Now let's look at what we have learned in a different way. I always prefer to learn things in different ways to help me reinforce what I have learned. So let's go back to where we began. Remember those three shapes I showed you: the shapes that are contained within the Major scale that we learned. I will include the fingerings below each note as well. From here on out I will denote the 1 3 4 (stretch) by putting parenthesis around it. (1 3 4) They are as follows:

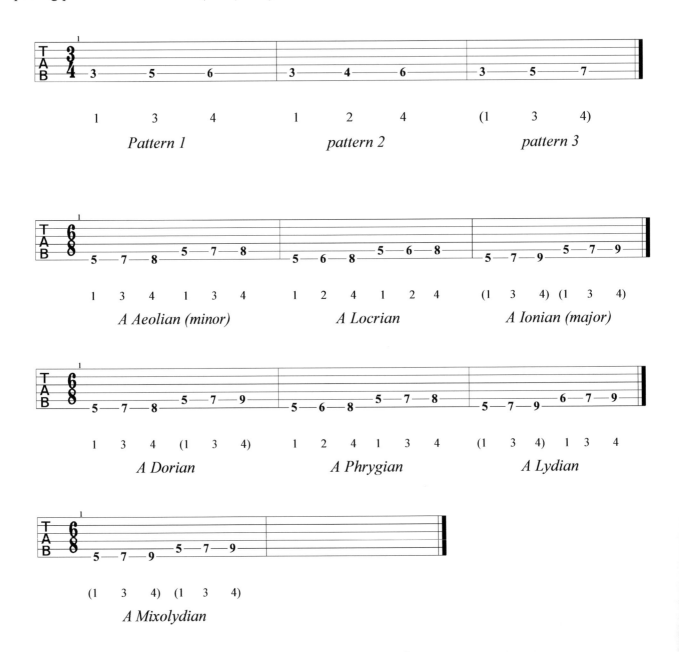

**I had written those all in the key of A. We know this because that is the note that each mode began on. So let's analyze how the three shapes fit together.**

We can see that the Aeolian scale consists of pattern 1 on the E string and again on the A string. So if we look at it as 1 3 4 on the E string and 1 3 4 on the A string we know that we are in the Aeolian (minor) mode. I'll make a little chart so you can visualize this a little easier.

| Mode | E String | A String | Fingering E | Fingering A |
|---|---|---|---|---|
| **Aeolian mode** | Pattern 1 | Pattern 1 | 1   3   4 | 1   3   4 |
| **Locrian mode** | Pattern 2 | Pattern 2 | 1   2   4 | 1   2   4 |
| **Ionian mode** | Pattern 3 | Pattern 3 | (1   3   4) | (1   3   4) |
| **Dorian mode** | Pattern 1 | Pattern 3 | 1   3   4 | (1   3   4) |
| **Phrygian mode** | Pattern 2 | Pattern 1 | 1   2   4 | 1   3   4 |
| **Lydian mode** | Pattern 3 | Pattern 2 (up one fret) | (1   3   4) | 1   2   4 |
| **Mixolydian** | Pattern 3 | Pattern 3 | (1   3   4) | (1   3   4) |

But wait, according to this chart Ionian mode and Mixolydian mode are the same. You are absolutely correct. This is because I only had us looking at the first six notes of the scale as opposed to all seven. The difference between Mixolydian and Ionian is the 7th note of each mode.

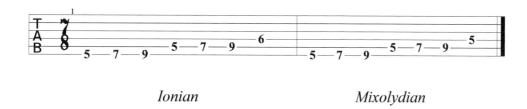

*Ionian*                    *Mixolydian*

Notice that they are the exact same until we get to the 7$^{th}$ note. Ionian has its 7$^{th}$ note one degree higher than the Mixolydian scale.

# A More Visual Approach

### *A quick word on these fretboard diagrams:*

When I display these fretboard diagrams I have purposely not labeled what fret they start out on. This is because they are simply *PATTERNS*. What fret they start on does not matter to us. We are only interested in the *PATTERN*.

Let's take a look at how these seven patterns look with our fretboard diagrams.

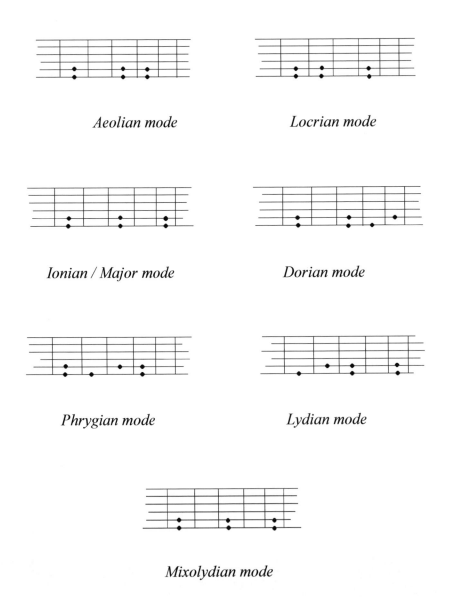

*Aeolian mode*              *Locrian mode*

*Ionian / Major mode*        *Dorian mode*

*Phrygian mode*              *Lydian mode*

*Mixolydian mode*

# Employing Octaves

Let's take the Aeolian/ Minor shape that consists of the fingering 1 3 4 on the E string and 1 3 4 on the A string. We know that if we wish to play in A minor all we have to do is play this shape starting on an A. So we can also look at the pattern like this if we, for the time being, don't think about the seventh note of the scale.

*A minor (with the 7<sup>th</sup> omitted)*

Notice that we only used the Aeolian shape yet we were able to change this into an eighteen note run by repeating the same shape three times with each shape starting on A. Another great advantage of looking at it this way is to realize how much of the fretboard we used. We just made a run by repeating the same shape that spans from the 5<sup>th</sup> fret all the way up to the 13<sup>th</sup> fret. Now we are beginning to use the whole fretboard and not stay within the little "boxes". And, this really took very little memory on our part at all. All we had to do was repeat a little six note shape and move it around to each root note.

Let's try it with something new. Let's say we want to play in G Phrygian. We know the Phrygian shape is fretted 1 2 4 on the E string and 1 3 4 on the A string. So all we have to do is start this shape on a G if we want to play G Phrygian mode.

*G Phrygian (with the 7<sup>th</sup> omitted)*

Again, all we did was take the six note pattern that we know to be the Phrygian mode and repeated it three times beginning on a G each time.

# And Yet One More Way to Look at What We Have Learned

This is more of a way to let you know what mode and key you are playing in. Let's just take our tried and true, old faithful, Aeolian / Minor pattern. We know that it is fretted 1 3 4 on the E string and 1 3 4 on the A string. So let's look at this pattern on three different pairs of strings.

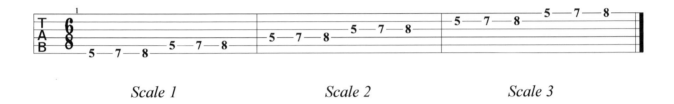

*Scale 1*                    *Scale 2*                    *Scale 3*

So now we see the exact same pattern on three different sets of strings. We know that this is not one scale but three *different* scales. So how can we tell what they are? Well, we know the shape. We know this shape to be the Aeolian / Minor mode. So all we have to do is figure out what note each one starts on. That's easy enough.

In the first measure the shape starts on the $5^{th}$ fret on the low E string. This is an A. So we know that the first measure is an A minor scale.

In the $2^{nd}$ measure we have the exact same pattern but it starts on the $5^{th}$ fret of the D string. We know that that note is a G so we are playing in G Aeolian / minor.

In the $3^{rd}$ measure we again have the same Aeolian / minor shape but it starts on the $5^{th}$ fret of the B string. The $5^{th}$ fret on the B string is an E. So we know that we are playing in E minor

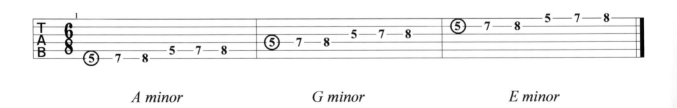

*A minor*                    *G minor*                    *E minor*

# Unlocking the True Power of Modal Theory

### (How to Never Run Out of Licks)

So now we are at least semi educated in music theory. There is so much more to learn but for our purposes we have covered 90% of what we are going to use in our metal genre. So let's take a look at how we can apply this to our playing and how we can multiply the number of licks in our arsenal, because we can never have too many licks.

Let's start with a nice little speedy lick that many guitarists use and sounds very cool. It is also not all that difficult to play at higher speeds. We will assume that we are playing over an A chord and we will choose to play the A minor scale because that always fits so well. We could have chosen any of the seven modes but let's start with A Aeolian because we are very familiar with it.

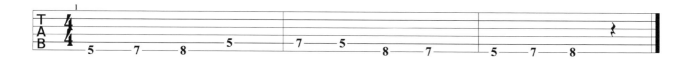

You can play this lick any way you like. Play it legato, picking, palm muted, etc. I like to play it by picking the first three notes while palm muting the strings followed by hammering and pulling off on the upper three notes and then back to picking and palm muting. Either way it can be a very cool sounding lick and you can play it any style you wish to.

So is that it? We have a cool lick and we only play it there and in that one key? Seems like quite a waste of a cool lick. So let's take the lick and play it in some different spots. We know all of the notes in the A minor scale so let's use the same pattern and just start it out on different notes within the A minor scale.

Here are just a few different ways that we can apply that cool lick to notes within the A minor scale.

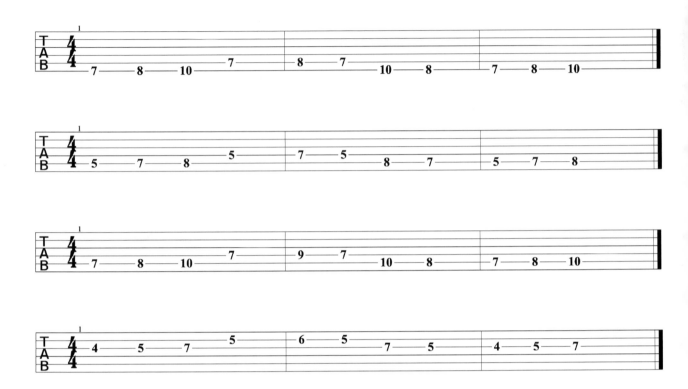

Notice that we are playing the exact same *pattern* but we are changing the starting note and playing the pattern diatonic to the A minor scale. The pattern is the same because we are looking at it as playing three notes going up followed by the 4th note, then 5th, then back to the 4th, then the original three notes down and up again.

So mathematically speaking, our instrument is roughly four octaves depending on what note we start on. There are seven notes in the scale. So we can take a lick, start it in seven different positions, and in four octaves. So we could turn one lick into 7 * 4 = 28. That's twenty eight different licks not counting the places where we could play the same notes but with different fingerings. That's not bad at all. By this math we could learn 10 licks and end up with 280 different licks. Not too bad at all!

Let's try another one. This one is quite a bit more advanced. Here is a nice lick in D minor that is built for speed. Again, you can play this lick either picking or legato or a combination of both. It sounds really cool either way and because of the way the picking is structured we can really get this one up to speed.

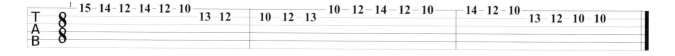

*D minor*

Now let's say we want to play that exact same lick in E minor. All we have to do is move the pattern back until we are in E minor. So it will look like this:

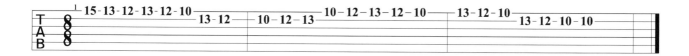

*E minor*

Now if we wanted to play the same lick in E Phrygian it would look like this:

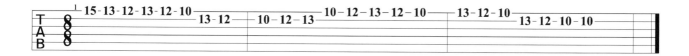

*E Phrygian*

# How Does This Modal Theory Relate To The Pentatonic Scale?

Remember when I told you that all scales are actually based off of the major scale? Well here I will show you an example. Let's take a look at a scale that I'm sure all of you know. It's probably the first scale that you learned as a budding young guitarist. It's the A minor Pentatonic scale. Here it is in both TAB and fretboard views:

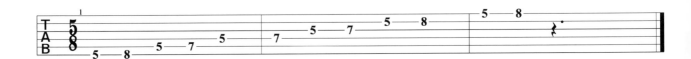

*Minor pentatonic*

Now you are probably very familiar with this scale. Since it is the A minor pentatonic scale let's take a look at our A Aeolian / minor scale that we have learned and compare the two.

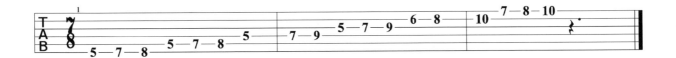

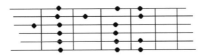

*Aeolian / minor*

They look pretty similar in shape. Can you tell what the differences are? Notice that if we remove the $2^{nd}$ and the $6^{th}$ notes from the A minor scale we get the A minor pentatonic. Or, conversely, if we add two notes to the A minor pentatonic scale we get the A minor scale.

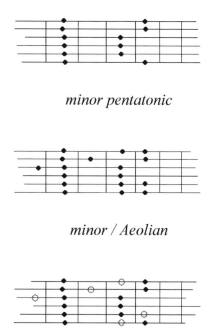

*minor pentatonic*

*minor / Aeolian*

*Minor / Aeolian with the $2^{nd}$ and $6^{th}$ notes as circles*

So I started us off by learning the seven patterns of the major scale. Now we know that if we take that scale and subtract the $2^{nd}$ and $6^{th}$ notes we will end up with the minor / Aeolian scale.

There is another school of thought by many guitar instructors that you should start by learning the pentatonic scale and add 2 notes so that you end up with the minor / Aeolian scale. I started that way as well and it only confused me when I learned the major scale. Pentatonic has five notes. How do I know which ones to add? Pentatonic only has five patterns. Why do I have to learn seven now? I was confused. *(The Pentatonic scale only has five patterns because there are only five notes in the scale)...* I know you knew that already though.

# A Quick tutorial about Keys

I have mentioned which modes to use when we are in a certain "key". Perhaps you are already able to ascertain what key the background is in but if not, I will very briefly go over a few basics. There are some specific ways that conventional theory explains it but I will bypass those for the sole reason that many times in metal we do things that aren't very conventional. Also in metal we rely on power chords almost exclusively. This takes much of the more advanced theory out of the equation. Let's take a look at a nice easy way to understand keys.

Let's start by taking a look at the A minor scale as it looks across the entire fretboard.

*A minor*

Looking at this scale we can make a few different power chords.

**A    C    D    E    F    G**

As we look at the scale placed across the entire fretboard, visualize the possible chords. In all reality we could play the B chord as well and our scale would still "mostly" fit. It's not "technically" correct but we're playing metal and we don't have to follow all of the rules all of the time.

So as long as we are relying on power chords, we could play any of the chords within the scale. We can also play quite a few IV chords which are more chords that are contained in the scale. IV chords are the ones where you just bar two notes on the same fret. They contain the 1st and 4th note of the scale. They have a nice metal type tone to them.

# Method Number Two

### *(How to determine what notes to play in a solo)*

This is the method that I commonly use. It's quick. It's easy. It isn't hard to learn but it loses *some* of its value when we get into harmonic minor scales and more advanced chord progressions that employ the 3$^{rd}$ tone of the chord thus making them major, minor, diminished, augmented, etc. But a great way to start is to listen to the backing track that you will be playing over. Have the backing track playing when you try to find the key.

While the backing track is playing slowly slide your finger up the neck on the low E string until you hit a note that sounds "correct" to you. Most often this will be the root note of the scale that the background is in. Notice that you can just hold this note as the background changes but it still sounds "right" to you. It is still in tune. Make sure to listen to the backing track. Also, more times than not, this note is also the first note in the chord progression.

**Treat this note as your root note and start your scale of choice from there.**

Not much thinking here. I sort of like this method because we can quickly find a mode to play in without having to sit down and analyze the chord progression. If nothing else, once you learn how to use this method you will be able to determine the key that the song is in purely by ear. Now whether this key should be major, minor, diminished, etc, might take a little bit of experimenting on our part but that's ok. Many times we get lucky on our first try. We also sometimes stumble to a mode that we would not have thought of playing but really enjoy the sound. The important part to this method is learning to use our ears as we slowly slide our finger up the E string and being able to determine the note that works for all of the chords. It's easier than you would think, so give it a try.

# Some Advantages to Learning Theory the Harder Way

I feel that there are many advantages to learning music theory the "harder way". When I say the harder way, I mean learning the minor scale before you master the pentatonic scale. Now, this probably only applies if you knew that you were planning to play metal / shred. If I had a student that wanted to play blues or country music then I would definitely start them out with the pentatonic scale.

### *The Minor Scale Begs To Be Divided Into Three Notes Per String Shapes.*

Three note per string shapes lend themselves very well to fast runs and shred guitar. The predictable picking patterns greatly help you to build speed. Now the pentatonic scale can also be divided into three notes per string but this comes at a price. The stretches involved can be very difficult to reach below the 9$^{th}$ fret or so. On the higher frets this can sound really cool though.

### *I Found It Much Easier To Subtract A Note Than To Add One.*

Now this is just me and you could be different. Do whatever works best for you! One of the advantages that I found was I would get the major scale so ingrained into my playing that when I tried to play the pentatonic I would sometimes forget to take out one of the notes. So I was essentially switching randomly between the pentatonic scale and the minor / Aeolian scale. And you know what? It sounded really cool the majority of the time. I like being able to add a note to the pentatonic scale on occasion without even trying to and having that extra note enhance the pentatonic scale.

### *I Believe It to Be Much Easier To Learn the Seven Patterns First*

I found it much easier to just learn the seven patterns first as opposed to learning the five pentatonic patterns and then basically just putting them to the side and learning the seven patterns that I needed in order to play this style of music.

This brings up another point. If you want to play shred, classically flavored, heavy metal music, don't spend your practice time learning something that won't apply to your playing right now. If you can't play an arpeggio yet and you are practicing some obscure jazz scale that your teacher told you to because it will make you a better, "well rounded" player you should ask yourself: Is this what I want? Do I need this at this point of my talent level? Or are there other techniques I should be focusing on first?

I love blues guitarists. I love guitarists like Eric Clapton, BB King, and David Gilmore. They are awesome, great, unbelievable, masters at the guitar. But do you think they know much about the theory we are learning here? Do you ever hear them sweep picking and playing classical sounding licks? I would even be willing to bet that if you are reading this book you can play quite a few licks at a much higher speed than any of them. Can we just admit that they play a different style of music than we do? And, for the style of music that they play they are at the top of their craft. I could listen to them in amazement for hours.

My point is this. Do you think they spent much time learning our style of music? Did their teachers tell them that they had to learn all of these scales, modes, and techniques that we know so they could be better "well rounded" players? They play what they love, and my advice to you is to do the same. I am in no way at all telling you not to branch out and learn different styles. On the contrary, I would recommend that you do. But if there is some technique or style that you really want to learn, learn that first! In essence, learn what you want to play, not what you don't.

# The Harmonic Minor Scale

Ok, I at least have to glance over the harmonic minor scale. In our metal / shred genre of music this is a pretty important scale. This particular scale is one of the most evil, classical, sad sounding scales that I know of. Many shred players take advantage of it and you can instantly hear the different tone that it is famous for.

The harmonic minor scale is only one note different than the minor scale we have previously learned but that one note makes a huge difference. The different note is called the *raised 7<sup>th</sup>*. The raised 7<sup>th</sup> is just what it says. Take the 7<sup>th</sup> note of the Aeolian/minor scale and move it up one fret. Here it is in both TAB and fretboard view. I have circled the raised 7<sup>th</sup> notes.

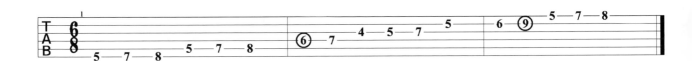

*A Harmonic minor*

Notice that it is exactly the same as our Aeolian / minor scale except for the circled notes which are one fret higher (*raised*).

Here is the A Harmonic minor scale in another popular fingering. The last one had the root note on the E string while this one has the root note on the A string. Again, I have circled the raised 7<sup>th</sup>.

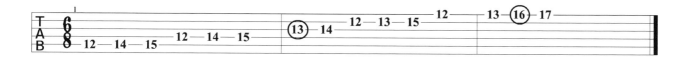

*A Harmonic minor*

Now, try playing these notes over an A chord and you will hear the eerie, evil, classical tone it invokes. And remember, all we did was change one note from our Aeolian / minor scale. That one note sure makes a difference though, doesn't it?

In a little bit I will show you two very usable fingerings for this scale that will greatly help you cover more fretboard real estate. The fingerings are also built for speed and are easy to visualize. But first let's go over something that really surprised me when I was learning theory.

So all we did was raise the 7<sup>th</sup> note of the minor scale and it sounds really cool and was easy to perform. In fact, it sounds so cool that it seems like it's a totally different scale. And you know what? It is a totally different scale. And since it is a different scale, do you know what we can do with it? We can apply modal theory to it! This means that we could use the exact same process as we did with the major scale and make seven different modes out of this scale! See how fast our knowledge of scales is increasing! In our genre of metal music the most used mode of the harmonic minor scale other than the 1<sup>st</sup> is the 5<sup>th</sup> mode. This mode is labeled the Phrygian dominant scale.

# The Phrygian Dominant Scale

The 5th mode of the harmonic minor scale is similar to the Phrygian mode that we have learned already. So Phrygian is the fifth mode when we start from the Aeolian / minor scale. And, remember how we liked the tone of the Phrygian mode? It was nice and dark, eerie, and sad. And then we learned the harmonic minor scale. And that was even more dark and sad. Well now we are taking harmonic minor scale, which is already dark and sad, and using the Phrygian mode of it, which as you can imagine, turns this into arguably the most eerie, sad, evil, minor, classical sounding scale there is. And the name of it is **Phrygian Dominant**. I didn't name it. It already had this name. Harmonic minor Phrygian mode would make more sense to me but hey, I don't make the rules, I just play by them.

So perhaps from what you have learned already you can figure out how to play this mode. If not, let's figure it out here. Let's start with what we just learned, the Harmonic minor scale in the key of A. Here it is to refresh your memory:

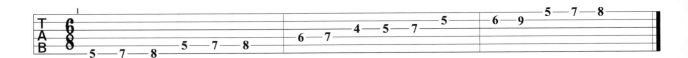

*A Harmonic minor*

So, one real easy way would be to count the notes from the root note. And we find that the 5th note in the scale is the 7th fret on the A string. The 7th fret on the A string is an E. So we could play this exact same scale but instead of playing it over an A chord we play it over an E chord. Now the scale would be E Phrygian dominant.

# Wait, I'm Confused? Say That Again About The Phrygian Dominant.

Yes, it is difficult to understand at first. Let's recap. If we take the A Harmonic minor scale that we just learned and play it over an A chord, we would label it A Harmonic minor.

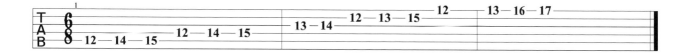

*A Harmonic minor / E Phrygian Dominant*

If we play this over an E chord as opposed to an A chord, then the name of the scale changes from A harmonic minor to E Phrygian dominant?

## Why?

Ok, when we are playing this over an E chord, of course we can still *think* of this as A Harmonic minor. We are playing the exact same notes as the A harmonic minor scale. Nothing has changed. How can the name of the scale change like that then? The answer is that something did change. The chord we were playing over. We changed keys. We played the same scale but because we are playing it in a different key then that changes how we name and *think* of our scale.

This is one of the main reasons that I have been referencing everything to the A Aeolian / minor scale. If the 5th mode of A harmonic minor is the same as E Phrygian dominant then bingo. We can play those notes in the key of A or E and they will both be in tune. Sure, one will sound darker than the other but we will be in tune none the less. And since so many metal songs are written in E or A, we can get a lot of mileage out of this scale.

Here I will attempt to show it to you in a way that will help reinforce what we just learned. This is the A Harmonic minor scale:

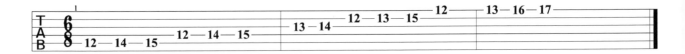

*A Harmonic minor*

We want to play the 5<sup>th</sup> mode of it (Phrygian dominant) in the key of E. So we look at this pattern and count to the 5<sup>th</sup> note in the scale which is E. (14<sup>th</sup> fret on the D string) Now we can conclude we are already playing E Phrygian dominant. Let me fill in the lower notes of the scale so you can see it on the low E string as well:

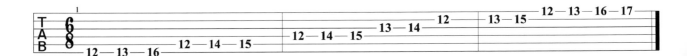

*E Phrygian dominant*

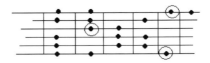

Remember, Phrygian and Phrygian dominant are two separate scales because of the raised 7<sup>th</sup>. So let's compare the two: Phrygian and Phrygian dominant respectively and you will see the similarities.

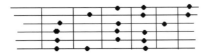

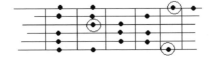

# Harmonic Minor Picking Patterns

Here are two great patterns for playing the harmonic minor scale. They both cover a lot of the fretboard and there are quite a few guitarists who rely on these two patterns almost exclusively when playing the harmonic minor scale and its 5th mode the Phrygian dominant scale. Let's start with pattern #1 in A Harmonic minor. I know, I lean rather strongly towards starting us out in the key of A.

*A Harmonic minor*

And here is pattern # 2. This pattern is shown in the key of E Harmonic minor.

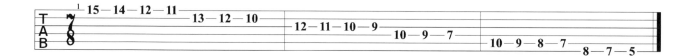

*E Harmonic minor*

Pattern # 1 is in A Harmonic minor. This is true when we are playing in the key of A. But, if we were to play this fingering when in the key of E, then it becomes the E Phrygian dominant scale.

# One Scale, Seven Patterns, Seven Different Names

This part of theory has always proved to be confusing for many guitarists. I know I had a hard time understanding it at first. I'll do my best to explain it as simply as possible. Let's start off with our A Aeolian / minor scale.

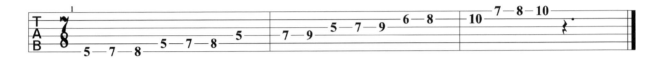

*A Aeolian / minor*

We know by now that this is the A minor scale. We know this because we know the pattern and the pattern starts on the 5th fret of the low E string which is an A. We also know because it is the A minor scale, the notes are: A B C D E F G and then it repeats.

Now let's go over the seven names part. If we play this in the key of A we name this scale A minor. But, if we were to play it in the key of B we would call it B Locrian. If we play it in C then we would name it C Ionian / major. I'll make a little chart.

| Key | Mode Name |
|---|---|
| A | A    Aeolian |
| B | B    Locrian |
| C | C    Ionian |
| D | D    Dorian |
| E | E    Phrygian |
| F | F    Lydian |
| G | G   Mixolydian |

We are still playing the exact same notes as on the previous page. So how can it have 7 different names? We use different names because we would be way too confused if we said we were playing G Mixolydian over an A chord. Or, if we said we were playing B Locrian over an A chord. Now we could say that and we would be entirely correct in saying it. Actually, if you want to show off to your friends, tell them that the solo you just played was in F Lydian. They will think you are a master of Music theory. They will wonder how you could memorize all of those scales. But we didn't. We were only playing the A minor scale. Your friend might even already know this scale. He just does not understand the terminology or how to apply modal theory to what he already knows to further his knowledge and musicianship.

So, put some time in learning the concepts of music theory. You don't need to master every single aspect of it. However, you should at the very least be able to apply music theory to the style of music that you play. As you can see, the basics of theory are not that difficult. It takes a little time to learn the 7 patterns but your playing will improve exponentially once you do.

I found that after I had learned the seven patterns everything made more sense to me. Previously I had known four of the patterns and ignored the other three. My knowledge of music theory never advanced. I didn't understand modes. I felt I had to memorize all of them as separate scales when the reality turned out to be that I only had to memorize one scale and its seven patterns. And, how would it even be possible to understand modes if you don't know all seven patterns? Trust me, it's not possible.

I will be coming back to music theory throughout the book. It is of my belief that no matter what cool new lick we learn, we should always try to analyze what scale or mode it is utilizing.

Now, let's move to the next section which is the technique and theory of arpeggios. To be a complete shredder, this is an absolute "must learn" technique!!

# ARPEGGIOS

Arpeggios, also known as sweep picking, might be one of the most enjoyable, satisfying techniques to play in all of shred guitar. The smooth, lightning speed transitions across a whole octave or more create a very identifiable tone. For many guitarists, learning arpeggios is the threshold between being accomplished and average. I don't think that I agree with that. There are many, many great guitarists who do not employ any arpeggio techniques. At least not the multiple note, wider ranging ones we will be learning here. However, for our metal / shred genre, the arpeggio is an awesome weapon to have included within our arsenal.

Sweep picking can take some time to learn. There really is no time table for this. Some instructors say 6 months of solid work. That is roughly how long it took me to play most of the shapes that we regularly use in our playing. And quite honestly, once I could perform most of the sweeps from every lesson I could find and playing all of my favorite players' arpeggios, I stumbled quite hard with them in my own music. I had all of these great arpeggios but how do I use them? I had no clue. I had spent a considerable amount of time learning this advanced technique, yet I could not employ them in my own playing. They never sounded as if they "fit". The part I was lacking was the theory portion. You can't play any arpeggio at any time. And they can actually sound pretty bad when played against the wrong chord.

One great thing about learning arpeggios is that they are an almost 50/50 split between technique and theory. You could know all the theory in the musical world but if you haven't learned the technique, you can't employ them in your playing. Conversely, you could learn them, as I did, and be able to perform the technique but unable to know how to use them so that they are in tune with the chord you are playing against. Wanting to use arpeggios in my playing is what forced me to begin learning music theory.

# A Few Tips When Learning How to Sweep Pick

## *We Will Start By Learning Six of the Nine Basic Shapes*

With these six different shapes we will be well on our way to performing arpeggios. These six shapes will give us a sturdy base to stand on. There are many more shapes that we can learn but let's start with these six. There are nine "must know" shapes and we will learn the other three after we have the first six down.

## *Strive to play each and every note perfectly and cleanly!*

I know I've said this before but when playing arpeggios this rule elevates to a new level. This is a difficult technique to learn and even good players tend to get sloppy with them at times. Some of the shapes that we will learn are easier to play cleanly than others. Don't think that just because you learn one of the shapes that you don't have to put in a little time learning others.

## *The Picking Hand Is What You Will Struggle With!*

You must realize that when learning this technique your picking hand will be the problem. Concentrate on your picking hand when learning this technique. Arpeggios are all about timing and synchronization. You must learn how to strike *and* fret the note simultaneously while at the same time not letting excess string noise occur.

## *Eliminating String Noise Is Extremely Important!*

Arpeggios can sound very sloppy if we do not concentrate on eliminating excess string noise. This technique is all about timing and having both of our hands married. The ringing of overlapping tones when not performed properly can ruin the arpeggio. It will just sound like a poorly executed chord. There are two ways to eliminate this string noise and you must learn to master them both! The two ways are quite easily enough labeled: Your Right Hand and Your Left Hand.

### Realize That Arpeggios And Theory Go Hand In Hand!

Arpeggios can be very difficult to use practically without any musical theory knowledge. Even if every note within the arpeggio is contained within your desired scale or mode it will not always sound pleasant. So as important as learning the technique portion is, learning the reasons and general rules about how to coax arpeggios to fit within our desired musical application is just as important.

### Arpeggios Are Chords!

The definition for an arpeggio is "broken chord" or "To play the individual notes of a chord in sequence". Yeah, yeah, yeah… I know this. They are chords played one note at a time… Blah, blah, blah…. The important part of the definition is not that they are notes played in succession. The important part, that both definitions denote, is that arpeggios are *chords*. And although we will be thinking of individual notes at times in this lesson, we are actually learning how to play chords over backing chords.

### We must pay attention to timing as well!

I have been thru this as well. We can practice an arpeggio until it sounds great. We can play it very fast, clean, and we know how to make it fit "in tune" within our desired tonic framework. Now when we try to employ this arpeggio in a solo, we find that we can only reproduce our great arpeggio at one speed or meter. We can't play it faster or slower without making mistakes. We must practice arpeggios at different speeds and tempos. When an arpeggio is played cleanly, with no excess string noise, and is "in time" with our background rhythmic framework, there are very few techniques in metal that sound more classical and virtuosic.

# Our First Basic Arpeggio Shape

Many guitar instructors will start you out with learning a three string arpeggio. I was always more adventurous and immediately sought out the more difficult arpeggios when I was first learning them. I'll touch more on that and my reasons for starting you off this way later.

Let's take a look at our first and one of the most popular arpeggio shapes in metal music. For now, let's just learn the technique and how to play it cleanly. We will start adding in the theory portion as we continue throughout the lesson. Here is our first shape. And it is in the key of…..A minor again? Yep, that's right, A minor.

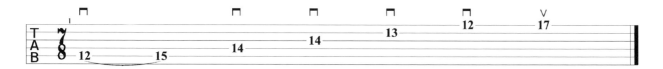

*A minor ascending*

Play the above exercise a few times to get the pattern under your fingers. For right now just concentrate on the pattern and the picking directions. Notice that this lick employs all down picks except for the very last note.

**As we begin to learn the technique of sweep picking, pay very strict attention to the picking directions and any hammer-ons or pull-offs that are used in these exercises. There are alterations to these picking patterns but for now let's just learn some of the easier and more practical ways of executing them.**

# Let's take a look at the descending version of the A minor arpeggio.

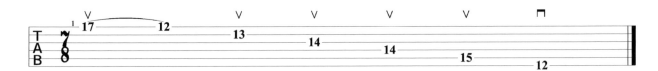

*A minor descending*

Again, pay strict attention to the picking pattern. Notice that this exercise is all up strokes except for the last note in the sequence.

Now let's tie them together and give us a very popular arpeggio to practice.

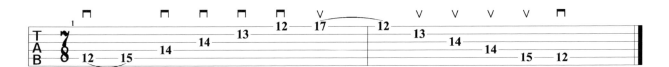

*A minor root position*

That is the first arpeggio we will learn. The A minor / Aeolian arpeggio is used very often in metal and can be used in many different situations.

Here is the pattern in fretboard view to help us visualize it better:

For now, we will only be concentrating on technique. So just remember that this particular arpeggio that we are starting with is A minor. We will go over the theory later.

# Now Let's Analyze the Full A minor Shape.

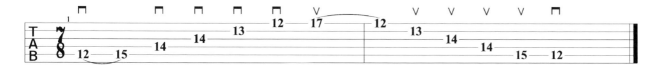

*A minor root position*

The notes seem easy enough to play. The difficult part is to not allow each individual note that we just played to ring out. We must play each note separately and distinctly by muting each note immediately after sounding them. Let's take a look at some of the technical areas that most, if not all, guitarists struggle with initially.

## *The Picking Hand*

**Palm Muting**

We must mute the strings with our picking hand to prevent the notes from ringing together. Remember, an arpeggio is the notes of a chord played one at a time. If we let each note ring out we are not really playing an arpeggio. We are playing a chord.

**Pick Angle**

We must pay close attention to our pick angle and make sure that the angle is great enough so it feels as though we are "slicing" through the strings. If our pick angle is not great enough, "flat picking" will tend to get the pick caught or hung up, causing the individual notes to not sound distinct and uniform while also hindering our timing.

**Keep Your Picking Hand Moving**

Our picking hand must stay in motion at all times. We cannot just hit a note, stop the pick, hit another note and so on. Our hand must move at speed that is determined by the speed of the arpeggio. Don't let the motion come to a halt

## Keep Your Picking Hand Firm

Attempt to keep the fingers that hold your pick locked in place. Your wrist, although it will roll slightly, should also remain firm. Not locked in place but firm.

## Pay Close Attention to the Picking Directions.

In your future you will learn many different arpeggios and ways to pick them. In our first examples I believe that the picking patterns that I have chosen and displayed are some of the easiest and most practical picking patterns to use. For now, play these arpeggios exactly as I have written them.

## *The Fretting Hand*

## Let Up On The Pressure Immediately After Fretting The Note.

Half of the muting technique with arpeggios involves our fretting hand. We must ease up on the pressure we apply to fretting each note immediately after sounding them so that any ringing will stop.

## Then Palm Muting Takes Over.

To play arpeggios cleanly, only one note can be sounded at a time. As soon as the note is sounded we must ease the pressure to mute the note with our fretting hand followed by completely lifting the finger off of the fretboard and letting our picking hand take over the noise reduction duties via palm muting.

## Rolling

When two notes are located on the same fret we must use a rolling motion with our fretting hand. When done correctly we will be able to sound one note while muting the others. This is a difficult technique to get accustomed to and will take a little time to master but once we learn it we are well on our way.

# Root Position Minor Arpeggio
## (1ˢᵗ, 3ʳᵈ, 5ᵗʰ)

*The root notes are the A's.*

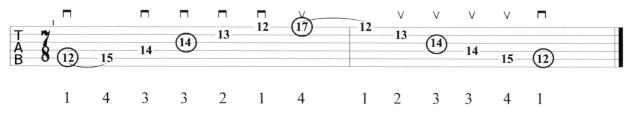

*I have included the fingerings below the TAB.*

## Let's look at what areas might be a problem for us.

The first two notes are easy enough. We only have to pick the first note. However, keeping our pick moving through this hammer-on without stopping the motion can prove to be a challenge.

The next two notes we have to bar our third finger to play them. This is where the rolling of the third finger comes into play.

The next two notes are easy enough. We just need to concentrate on playing them cleanly by lifting our fretting hand and also employing palm muting with our picking hand.

The last note in the measure and its pull off to the E is tricky for two reasons. One, this is where we change from all down strokes to all up strokes. Two, we again have to keep the picking hand in motion even with a direction change. From there on we come across the same issues as before but in a descending manner.

## *Now Practice the A minor Arpeggio!!*

We must now practice this technique. This can take a little bit of time before you are able to play it cleanly with any amount of speed.

Again, strive to play this cleanly. Practice it many times until you are able to play it cleanly without putting much thought into it.

We want to have this lick learned so well that when we want to play an A minor arpeggio we don't think about any of the notes involved. We just automatically sweep this pattern.

After some time, this arpeggio will begin to flow smoother, cleaner, and quicker. The main thing we are trying to accomplish is to just get one arpeggio under our belt that we can play well enough to understand the technical aspects of the technique. Each subsequent arpeggio we will learn will begin to seem easier and make more sense. There will also be less learning time involved in the process.

**Now Keep Practicing This Shape Until It Becomes Second Nature To You!**

# A Quick Word about Arpeggio Theory

I will delve deeper into arpeggio theory throughout this book, but for right now let's just gloss over some basics.

Most arpeggios are structured such that every other note in the scale is sounded. So in our case of the A minor arpeggio these notes would be the 1$^{st}$, 3$^{rd}$, and 5$^{th}$ notes of the A minor scale. I'll make a little chart to help demonstrate this.

*A minor scale*

| Note | A | B | C | D | E | F | G |
|--------|-----|---|-----|---|-----|---|---|
| Number | **1** | 2 | **3** | 4 | **5** | 6 | 7 |

So in our A minor arpeggio the notes are A, C, and E. Not surprisingly, these are also the notes that make up an A minor triad.

Looking at this chart and knowing the notes diatonic to the A minor scale, we can deduce that we can play these notes in three different orders. These different orders are called "inversions". Their orders are: A C E, C E A, and E A C. These are labeled root position, 1$^{st}$ inversion, and 2$^{nd}$ inversion respectively.

*A minor*

| Inversion | Order | Notes |
|-----------|-------|-------|
| **Root position** | 1, 3, 5 | A, C, E |
| **1$^{st}$ Inversion** | 3, 5, 1 | C, E, A |
| **2$^{nd}$ Inversion** | 5, 1, 3 | E, A, C |

# First Inversion Minor Arpeggio

## (3rd, 5th, 1st)

This is our 1st inversion minor arpeggio. This contains the same notes as before but the order is different. As you have guessed the arpeggio is in A minor. I will again display the proper fingerings below the TAB and circle the root notes.

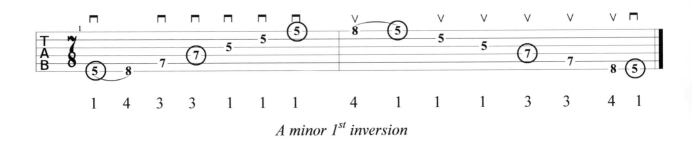

*A minor 1st inversion*

**And again, let's look at where the problem areas might be located.**

Now with this inversion, the picking hand is pretty much identical to the last arpeggio we learned so this shouldn't give us any more difficulties than the other one.

The problem that stands out with this inversion is that we have to bar two strings followed by a bar on three strings. This can be a tricky technique. This is where we have to "roll" our fingers that we are using to bar the notes. In this case it is our 3rd finger followed by our 1st finger. Without "rolling", the notes will ring together and we are all of a sudden playing a chord as opposed to the arpeggio that we were attempting to execute.

# Second Inversion Minor Arpeggio
## (5th, 1st, 3rd)

This is our 2nd inversion minor arpeggio. This is an outstanding arpeggio to learn for a couple of reasons, number one being that we do not have to bar any notes in the arpeggio. This makes it much easier to play cleanly. The second reason is that, in its most basic form, we can start it out with our pinky, which gives us different options when compared to the others. Let's take a look at it. Again, I will include the proper fingerings below the TAB and circle the root notes.

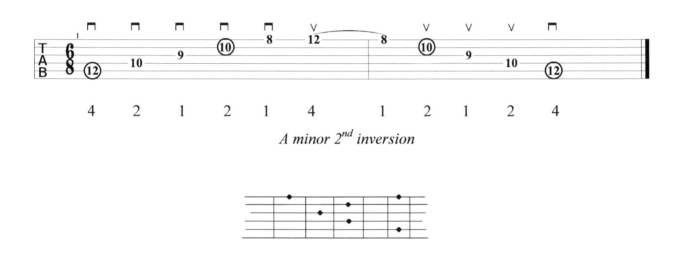

*A minor 2nd inversion*

So what are the problems we will have with this arpeggio? The answer is not as many problems as the others. We don't have to bar any notes, which is always nice from a players' standpoint. Our picking hand is performing roughly the same motion as the others. All we really have to concentrate on is our fretting hand, provided that our picking hand is making a nice smooth motion. This arpeggio helps us to concentrate on lifting our fret hand fingers immediately upon striking the note to avoid ringing.

# The Minors

Now that we have those three shapes under our belts let's learn the rest of the minor arpeggios.

**We're all done! We've already learned them all!**

*Seriously, that's it? We know every single minor arpeggio known to man?*

Of course we haven't learned every single one. But, we have learned the base. These three shapes that we just learned can go a very long way in our playing. I will expand on these later in the book but for now bask in the joy that you now know the three basic "must know" shapes for minor arpeggios.

Let's recap and see them all in TAB and Fret form.

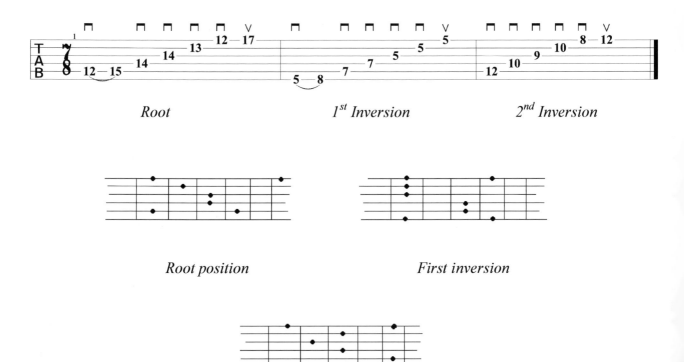

*Root*　　　　　*1ˢᵗ Inversion*　　　　　*2ⁿᵈ Inversion*

*Root position*　　　　　*First inversion*

*Second inversion*

# Now it's Time for Us to Move Up To the Majors!

So we have them down now and we're moving up to the major leagues? No, I'm talking about learning the 3 arpeggio inversions based on the major scale. And just as before when we learned 3 minor shapes, we will be learning 3 major shapes.

**The major arpeggio is the same as the minor arpeggio but the 3$^{rd}$ is raised.**

## *Root Position Major Arpeggio*
### *(1$^{st}$, 3$^{rd}$, 5$^{th}$)*

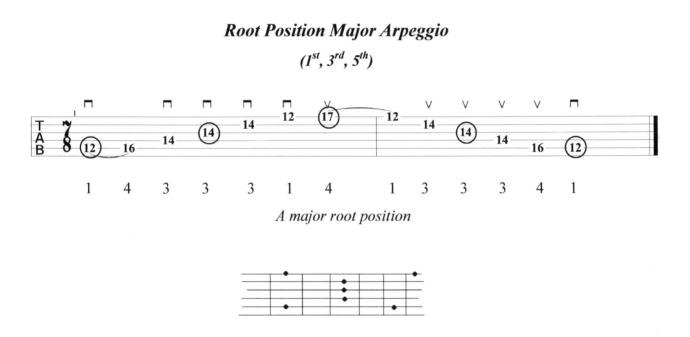

*A major root position*

Now when you play this, don't only think that you are learning a new shape. Think of this arpeggio as the *Major* version of our root position A minor arpeggio. It is the same except for the 3$^{rd}$ tone in the scale, which is raised. For now, work on being able to play the A major arpeggio cleanly. As before, pay close attention to the picking directions and the fingerings as well.

The difficult part with this inversion is the dreaded bar! We have to bar three strings this time with our 3$^{rd}$ finger. Work on "rolling" the 3$^{rd}$ so that each note is muted and does not ring out.

# The First Inversion Major Arpeggio
## (3<sup>rd</sup>, 5<sup>th</sup>, 1<sup>st</sup>)

This arpeggio is the sister of the 1<sup>st</sup> inversion minor arpeggio that we had learned earlier. Let's take a look at it in both forms. What key should we start it out in? Let's try it in A major this time. (*I know, another in the key A. You're shocked, right?*)

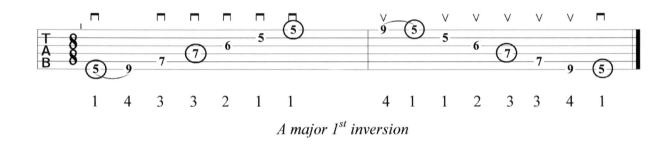

*A major 1<sup>st</sup> inversion*

Always remember that this is the sister of our 1<sup>st</sup> inversion minor arpeggio. It is the same except that the 3<sup>rd</sup> tone is raised. So what will be our difficulties when learning this arpeggio?

Again, we have to bar two notes and then after playing a note in between we have to bar two more notes. I hate having to bar notes!! It's so difficult to play them cleanly once we start increasing speed!! Oh well, there's no way around it, so I guess we should make sure that we learn how to bar notes within arpeggios and play them cleanly! It's difficult to do even when you have played them before so I think I'll go back and practice them on my own to be sure that I can still play them cleanly at fast speeds.

# The Second Inversion Major Arpeggio
## ($5^{th}$, $1^{st}$, $3^{rd}$)

And now we come to our last arpeggio of the major family, the $2^{nd}$ inversion major arpeggio. And as usual I will start it out in the key of A. Here is our A major $2^{nd}$ inversion arpeggio in both TAB and fretboard forms:

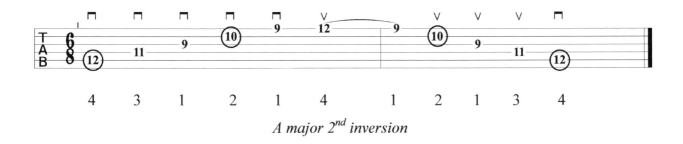

*A major $2^{nd}$ inversion*

And again, this is the sister arpeggio of the $2^{nd}$ inversion minor arpeggio. And just like that arpeggio, this one is great for us to play. No bars!! We can play these so much easier and cleaner without having to bar any notes.

# The Six Shapes We Have Learned Thus Far.

Now so far you have learned six shapes. And hopefully, you can play these six shapes ***cleanly*** at different speeds without thinking about the individual notes. To you, they are just six new licks that you have in your arsenal, or more accurately, six new "shapes" that you possess. And shapes can be much better to possess in your arsenal than licks. We can always turn those shapes and patterns into licks. But with licks, we have to dissect and revert them back into shapes in order to re-use them. Let's recap the six shapes we have learned.

*A minor Arpeggios*

*A major Arpeggios*

So now we have these six shapes. The important lesson that I was attempting to get across to you was that we must learn how to play these cleanly, quickly, accurately and effortlessly. If you can already play these shapes cleanly and at different speeds then that is fantastic. We don't have to worry about the technique portion of arpeggios and we can move on to the theory part so that we can learn how to use them and learn more of them.

# Do You Have These Six Shapes Learned?

Before we move on to learning more arpeggios and the theory behind them do you have these six shapes learned and are able to execute them at will? Once you get this technique down, learning more shapes becomes much easier and the amount of time you spend on them will begin to decrease.

Here are a just a few ways to practice these arpeggios in TAB form. Remember to strive for precision and trust me, the speed will follow.

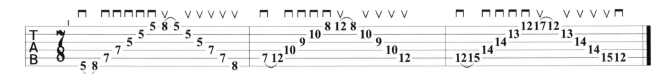

*A Minor*

*A Major*

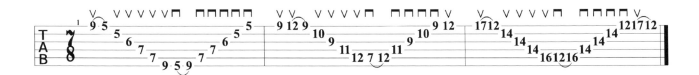

*A Minor*

*A Major*

# Playing These Arpeggios in Different Keys

Playing these arpeggios in different keys involves nothing more than playing the exact same shape but starting it out at a different spot on the fretboard. Let's take a look at the six shapes we have learned and I will circle their root notes.

*A minor Arpeggios*

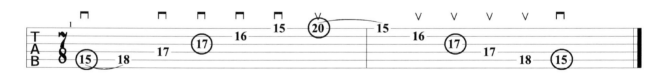

Root position          1<sup>st</sup> Inversion          2<sup>nd</sup> Inversion

So if we want to play any of these minor arpeggios in a different key all we have to do is start them out on the desired note and that's it. So, for instance, if we wanted to take our root position arpeggio and play it in the key of C, all we have to do is start it out on a C. I'll Tab out a C minor root position arpeggio for you.

*C minor (root position)*

Notice that it is the exact same pattern as our root position minor arpeggio but we started the *PATTERN* out on the fifteenth fret as opposed to the twelfth. Since the fifteenth fret on the A string is a C, this is a C minor arpeggio. Let's try a couple more to help reinforce this concept

Let's take a 1st inversion minor arpeggio and play it in E, thus making it an E minor 1st inversion arpeggio. Here is the A minor 1st inversion that we have already learned. I have circled the root notes. (The A notes)

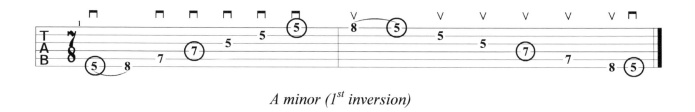

*A minor (1st inversion)*

So if we want to play an E minor first inversion arpeggio in E, then all we have to do is move the root note up until it starts on an E. So in this case let's move the root note up to the twelfth fret on the E string. The twelfth fret on the E string is an E. I would very much hope that you knew that! Here is the exact same shape but having the root note start on an E:

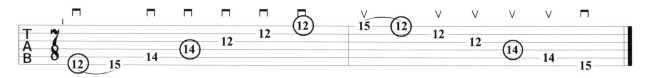

*E minor (1st inversion)*

See how easy this is? You don't have to remember all of these different arpeggios. All we have to remember are the "*shapes*" and on which fret to start them on.

# Three String Arpeggio Shapes

Now many guitar instructors would have started you out with these three string shapes and perhaps that would have been a better way for us to first learn them. But, I'm assuming that you are more like me and prefer to start out with the more difficult licks. This is how I learned them and I believe that it's the best way to learn. My thinking is that the most difficult part of learning how to execute arpeggios is learning how to fluidly sweep through them with your picking hand. The fretting hand usually evolves much more quickly than the fretting hand when it comes to arpeggios. So when we start out with five string arpeggios you down pick five notes as opposed to three, which to me seems like a much more efficient practice routine.

Whichever way you choose to learn is fine. There are no rules to learning and everyone is different. One thing you may notice is that, if you started with five and six string shapes like I did, you would think that playing three string shapes would be easy. I think they are easier after learning the other shapes but not as much as you would think. It still feels like we are learning a new technique even though we are just playing fewer notes than we did before.

Three string shapes sound very cool and are easy to move around the fretboard. You will learn to play these lightning fast and many times they can be much more usable than the longer arpeggios. They can have, when executed properly, an almost hypnotic effect when played against the proper chord. Now these three string shapes are the *EXACT* same as the longer shapes we just learned minus a few notes. All of the rules that we previously learned still apply.

# Three String Minor Arpeggios

### 3 String Root Position Minor Arpeggio
### (1ˢᵗ, 3ʳᵈ, 5ᵗʰ)

*A minor (root position)*

### 3 String First Inversion Minor Arpeggio
### (3ʳᵈ, 5ᵗʰ, 1ˢᵗ)

*A minor (1ˢᵗ inversion)*

### 3 String Second Inversion Minor Arpeggio
### (5ᵗʰ, 1ˢᵗ, 3ʳᵈ)

*A minor (2ⁿᵈ inversion)*

So those are your three 3 string minor arpeggio shapes. They are very fun to play and you can really get them up to a high rate of speed after a little bit of practice.

Now for the theory portion, all you have to remember for now is where the root note and the 3$^{rd}$ is. In the following TAB I have circled the root notes for you. And in this instance the root notes on all three shapes is the A note. This is because these three shapes are A minor arpeggios. The 3$^{rd}$ is boxed.

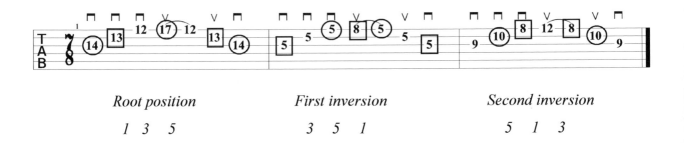

*Root position*      *First inversion*      *Second inversion*

*1   3   5*        *3   5   1*        *5   1   3*

Make sure to learn all three shapes so that you are able to play this arpeggio anywhere on the fretboard. If you only learn one or two of the shapes you are limiting yourself to just a section or two of the fretboard.

We can also make these a little bit more interesting to play by adding a bit of legato trills at the tops. I'll give an example showcasing the A minor root position 3 string arpeggio.

# Three String Major Arpeggios

And now we move on to our three string major shapes. We will go in the same order as we did with the minors so we will start with the three string A major root position arpeggio.

### 3 String Root Position Major Arpeggio
### (1st, 3rd, 5th)

*A major (root position)*

### 3 String First Inversion Major Arpeggio
### (3rd, 5th, 1st)

*A major (1st inversion)*

### 3 String Second Inversion Major Arpeggio
### (5th, 1st, 3rd)

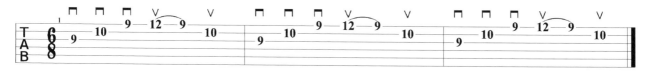

*A major (2nd inversion)*

# Inversion Practice

While we are learning these 3 string arpeggios let's also work on a useful little exercise that helps us to reinforce the different inversions of each arpeggio. All we have to do is play each inversion of an arpeggio in order. This can also be very useful to us in our solos. Let's start with A minor as usual.

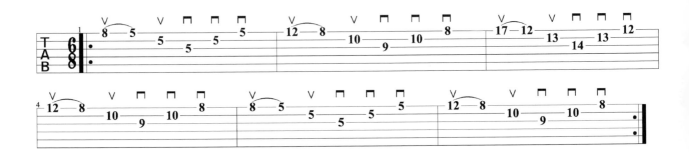

*A minor inversions*

The above exercise helps us with the theory portion of arpeggios as well as working on our position shifting technique. Let's try another one but this time we will practice the inversions in E minor.

*E minor inversions*

Try to practice these as smoothly and accurately as possible. Pay close attention to the position shifts as well.

# Diminished Arpeggios

So we have learned three minor shapes, three major shapes, and now we will move on to complete our knowledge of basic arpeggio shapes by learning the three diminished shapes. I have written these shapes out as four string arpeggios to help you with the fingerings. Diminished is the same as the minor but the 5th is flatted.

Diminished arpeggios, when used properly, achieve a very distinctive sound. Almost as if they are not supposed to fit within the scale. Diminished arpeggios beg to be "resolved". That is, they always sound as if they are a stepping stone to get to where you want to go. Let's take a look at the three shapes. I have included the suggested fingerings underneath each TAB.

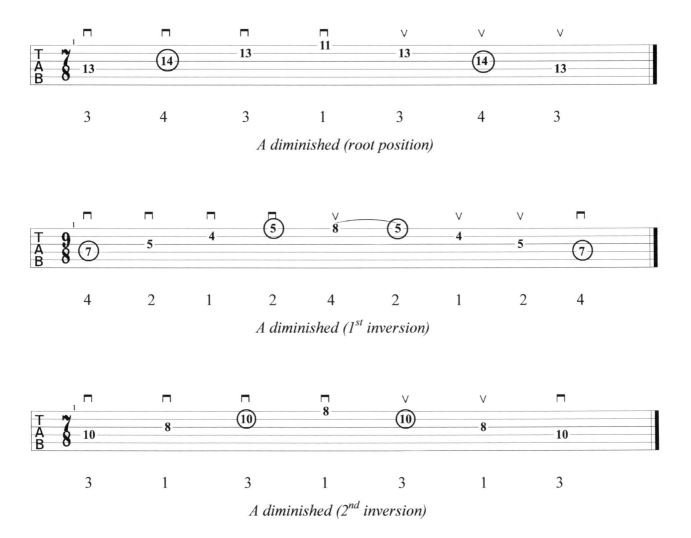

*A diminished (root position)*

*A diminished (1st inversion)*

*A diminished (2nd inversion)*

Now we have learned the nine basic shapes that nearly all arpeggios are built from. Learn these nine shapes well and be able to play them evenly, accurately, and smoothly. Many guitarists can get by with only these nine shapes and be able to execute an astonishing amount of arpeggio shredding.

In the next section we will begin to learn the theory behind playing arpeggios against a background. Arpeggio theory could be a whole book by itself so I will just go over the basics. But most importantly, I will explain how we can use them in the metal genre, particularly, how to use them in our soloing.

Arpeggios are not like regular single note runs. They are chords. And one of the easiest and most popular ways of using them is to just play the arpeggio that corresponds to the chord that you are playing over. This may seem mundane but trust me, it is not and you can get a lot of mileage out of this method.

So let's move on to the next section and learn how to apply some theory to the arpeggios that we have just learned.

# Arpeggio Theory

Arpeggio theory is not any different than our conventional music theory. Neither of them contradicts each other. The problem that we run into is that, since we are viewing arpeggios as licks containing multiple notes, they are a little trickier to fit into our solos. It's one thing to say that we can fit the individual notes into a certain key, but when we implement arpeggios into the same situations we must remember that they are actually chords. So even though all of the notes contained within the arpeggio are usable in your solo, when you play them as an arpeggio they don't always fit as you would expect. This is because they are chords. And if you played an A chord over an E chord it wouldn't sound very good.

So it's actually fairly easy to implement arpeggios into our playing. We just have to know a rule or two. Well, I guess I wouldn't call them rules. They are more like guidelines really. Rules are made to be broken. But let's start out the "classical way". Which scale should we start out with? I'll vote for A minor, and since I didn't see any other hands up, I win.

We know that the A minor scale contains the notes **A B C D E F G**.

With arpeggios there is one simple pattern that we have to remember. When we start out on the **Aeolian / minor** scale the order goes as follows:

*Minor,    Diminished,    Major,    Minor,    Minor,    Major,    Major*

We need to comprehend this because although we know that we can play the A minor arpeggio over an A note when we are in the key of A minor, we probably can't play a B minor arpeggio over the B note when the key is A minor. It will most likely clash. We would choose the B diminished arpeggio.

# A Chord / Arpeggio Scale Chart

I will make a little chart to help you visualize what I mean.

*For the key of A minor*

| Arpeggio | Corresponding Mode |
|----------|--------------------|
| *A minor* | *Aeolian/minor* |
| *B Diminished* | *Locrian* |
| *C Major* | *Ionian/Major* |
| *D Minor* | *Dorian* |
| *E Minor* | *Phrygian* |
| *F Major* | *Lydian* |
| *G Major* | *Mixolydian* |

Now what this chart says is that when we are in A minor, over an A note we would play an A minor arpeggio. Over the B note we would play a B diminished arpeggio. Over the C note we play a C major arpeggio. And so on…

So using the pattern **Min,    Dim,    Maj,    Min,    Min,    Maj,    Maj** we will know what arpeggio to play over each chord.

*Now I should mention something so that you don't get confused. Remember when I said that traditionally music theory bases everything off of the major scale? Well you will probably hear from other instructors that the pattern is:*

*Major, Minor, Minor, Major, Major, Minor, Diminished.*

*Which if you notice, this is absolutely correct when you start from the major scale. So as you can see, nothing is contradictory. I just view theory from a more "usable", "metal" approach.*

## So How Are We Supposed To Remember All Of That?

That would be tough wouldn't it? Some guitarists *seem* to be able to do it. Of course they would have to know the background chords prior to playing arpeggios over them unless they are amazing and can hear the chord, identify it, know what mode they are playing in, and then instantly choose the proper arpeggio to play over it. I can't do that. However what I can do, when writing a solo, is know the background chords and figure out which arpeggios to play. I rarely can figure them out on the fly unless I'm playing over the root chord, which many guitarists exploit greatly.

The truth is that we don't have to be able to instantly, on the fly, be able to improvise all of the different arpeggios that we know. We can write a solo, figure out which ones to play, and then when we perform them we look great. How many times are you just improvising solos when you don't know the backing chords anyways? Ok, maybe a lot. I do that too. Let me re-phrase. How many times are you just improvising solos that **utilize arpeggios**, when you don't know the backing chords **and are performing in front of an audience**? I really hope that you are able to get there someday. I hope I do as well. But for now, I'm very happy being able to play any arpeggio in tune with the background. I just work on it a little while you aren't listening. I greatly prefer to be very prepared before I play in front of an audience. Sure, I can improvise whenever I want to when I'm playing single notes. But, when you start throwing arpeggios into the mix, I would suggest that you work them out a little bit first before you start just throwing them into an improvised solo while you are onstage.

Most great guitarists are great because they practice before they perform. They seem to be able to play anything they want with ease. And they can. But I believe this is due to the fact that they put in hours of practice prior to a show.

# Arpeggio Theory Practice

Here is one way to practice our arpeggio theory. We can just pick an inversion and play all seven arpeggios of the scale in order. And remember if we are starting with the minor scale then the order is:

| Minor, | Diminished, | Major, | Minor, | Minor, | Major, | Major |
|:---:|:---:|:---:|:---:|:---:|:---:|:---:|
| G | A | A# | C | D | D# | F |

*G minor contains the notes G,   A,   A#,   C,   D,   D#,   F*

This exercise is in G minor and will utilize 4 string $1^{st}$ inversion arpeggios. Remember that the $1^{st}$ inversion arpeggio has the order of $3^{rd}$, $5^{th}$, $1^{st}$. However, since we are going to be playing 4 string arpeggios which start on a root note, our order will become $1^{st}$, $3^{rd}$, $5^{th}$, $1^{st}$.

This can be a great exercise to aide us in our quest for understanding the order or sequence that arpeggios are to be played.

# A Few Arpeggio Examples

So let's play just a few easy little arpeggios in sequence over some backing chords. This is all in A minor and you can see how you can switch between three different arpeggios as the chords change. Our backing chords will be (A   E   C) in that order. And looking back at our chart we can see that our arpeggios will be A minor, E minor, and C major respectively. So let's take a look at the TAB.

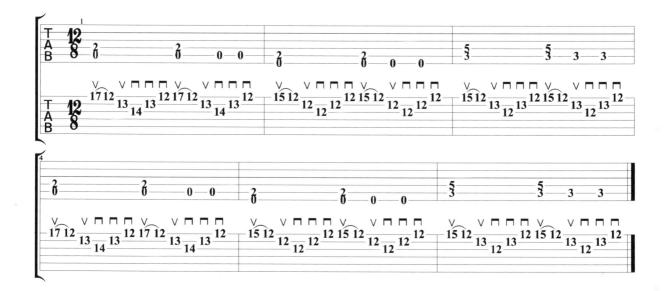

Notice that we stayed around the same position by using different inversions. Fingerings like this allow us to really play these quickly because we don't have to make any distant position changes.

# An E minor Example

The E minor scale contains the notes **E   F#   G   A   B   C   D**.

So using our chord scale of **min, dim, maj, min, min, maj, maj** we know what arpeggios to play over each chord. So if our background utilizes the chords E, B, A, C we would play E minor, B minor, A minor and C major respectively. This exercise sounds pretty classical and is good practice as well.

Key: *E minor*                    Chords: *E   B   A   C   E*

Notice that with this little exercise we also ran through a couple of different inversions as well. And as you know, the arpeggios that we played were:

| Chord | Arpeggio |
|-------|----------|
| *E* | *E minor* |
| *B* | *B Minor* |
| *A* | *A Minor* |
| *C* | *C Major* |

# A More Advanced Arpeggio with a Tap Lick

This is a very cool lick that I love to play. Not only does it sound really cool, it's very flashy and never fails to impress anyone that watches you perform it. I didn't invent this technique and to tell you the truth I have no clue who did, otherwise I would give them credit for their out of the box thinking.

Now this lick assumes that you pretty much have arpeggios down pat because we are going to add a tap at the end so that we can extend the arpeggio another note. This arpeggio takes some practice at first so make sure that you start it out slow and add speed as you become more comfortable with it.

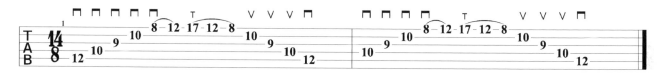

*A minor*

With this lick we have to execute the arpeggio going up, quickly tap the high note with our picking hand (2<sup>nd</sup> or ring finger) and as we are bringing our picking hand back in the position to finish the arpeggio we pull off one note to the E with our fretting hand and finish the arpeggio as usual.

Now as I said, this is an advanced lick and you really have to be able to execute arpeggios in your sleep before you attempt this but keep it in mind. When you can pull this off you have a lot of options to do some tapping licks at the top of your arpeggios.

# Another Advanced Arpeggio Lick

Let's try another advanced arpeggio technique. It's not quite as advanced as the last one but it is pretty tricky to pull off and it helps you to cover more of the fretboard. It's very usable in many situations and all it involves is becoming so familiar with two different inversions that you are able to switch / slide between them without missing a beat (literally). Again this is in A minor and all we are doing is playing the second inversion A minor arpeggio ascending and sliding up at the top note to go into a root position A minor arpeggio descending. Let's see the TAB.

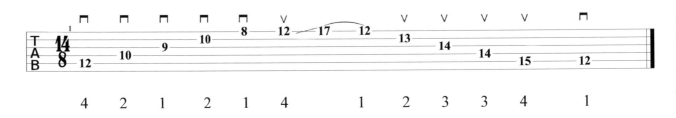

So obviously what makes this lick difficult other than being able to execute the arpeggio inversions is sliding up with your pinky and immediately pulling off to the E followed by completing the descending arpeggio in root position.

This is not impossible to play by any means but it is difficult to execute cleanly and in time. One of the advantages is that you are covering a lot of fretboard. From a low of the 8th fret all the way up to the 17th fret. And you cover all of that distance in the blink of an eye.

Again, as always, practice this slowly and precisely. You do not want to play any of these sloppy. A cleanly executed arpeggio is thought of by many to be the essence of shred guitar.

# The Diminished Scale

I can't in good conscience finish our arpeggio section without at least glancing over the diminished arpeggio again. Now I know that we went over the three diminished shapes earlier when we were looking at chord scales but this pattern seems a little different in feel and in functionality. This arpeggio is an integral part of the Harmonic minor scale and sounds incredibly eerie and unresolved.

The best part of this scale and its arpeggios is that it is a "symmetrical scale". This means that it repeats the same pattern across the whole fretboard so any memorization is unnecessary. Let's look at it on the fretboard first.

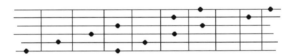

*Diminished Scale*

See what I mean when I say that it is a "symmetrical scale"? All we have to do is play every fourth fret. The beauty of it is that this scale is contained WITHIN the harmonic minor scale. And we loved how eerie that scale sounded. Well this scale is almost as if you removed the only normal notes and just left the eerie, evil, sad notes for us to play with. And, we don't even have to memorize anything. Every fourth note is all we need to know. Let me fill in the blanks with circles.

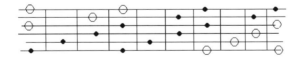

# The Diminished Scale / Arpeggio Continued

I just had to give a little bit of background on the diminished scale. If you tried playing through it, you can hear the very different tone it gives us. It sounds very outside of the scale even though it is actually diatonic to the harmonic minor scale. I will make this more clear in a little bit but first let's learn the easiest form of the diminished arpeggio; the three string diminished arpeggio.

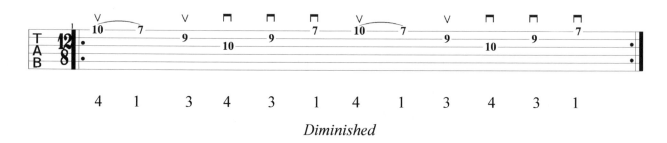

*Diminished*

Now when we are playing this particular arpeggio there are no root notes. I know that sounds strange. This is because it is contained *WITHIN* the harmonic minor scale. An easy way to know where to play this, or more accurately where to start this, is on the "raised seventh" of the harmonic minor scale that we learned earlier.

Let me TAB out a larger portion of the harmonic minor scale and I will circle the diminished scale notes to help you visualize the concept that I am trying to convey to you.

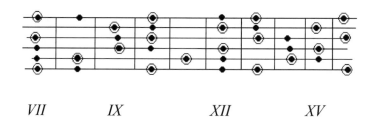

VII             IX             XII             XV

So you can see that all of the notes are the harmonic minor scale. But the notes that are circled (within the harmonic minor scale) are the notes that the diminished scale is comprised of. If you are still confused just know that you start out the diminished scale, which is every fourth note, on the raised 7th of the harmonic minor scale and you'll be fine.

# Arpeggios and Picking

One of the more difficult things to master when we are utilizing arpeggios is to mix in picking without altering the timing of the lick. We don't want to fall into the trap of only playing arpeggios up and down. We would like to be able to use arpeggios whenever we see fit and be able to switch to a different technique flawlessly.

The difficult part lies in our picking hand. To be able to switch from the smooth, rhythmic sweeping of an arpeggio to a quick picking lick takes some practice. Let's take a look at an example.

*A Minor*

The difficulty lies when we switch between the two techniques. Let's take a look at an inverse of a similar lick as well.

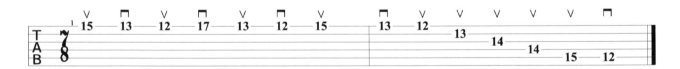

*A Minor*

The important thing to concentrate on is to attempt to keep the timing uniform. We want to execute our arpeggio at the same speed as the picked run.

Let's look at a few more examples.

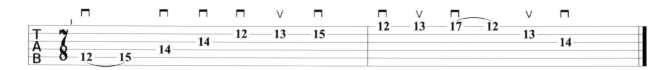

*A Minor*

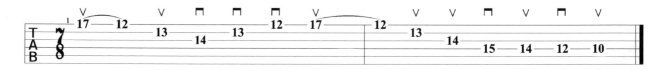

*A Minor*

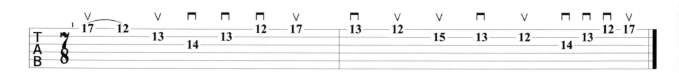

*A Minor*

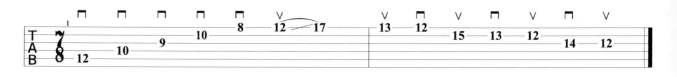

*A Minor*

These are just a few examples of the many possibilities of mixing the two techniques together. You should always have a set of 16th and 32nd note licks that you can add to arpeggios.

# Arpeggios and Tapping

I showed as an example a few pages ago of an arpeggio where the top note is tapped. This is a really fun technique to use once you get it down. Obviously you have to be able to play the arpeggio first before we can even think about adding on this technique but let's take a look at a few things we can do with this technique. Here is the basic arpeggio with a tap in A minor using the A minor $2^{nd}$ inversion arpeggio.

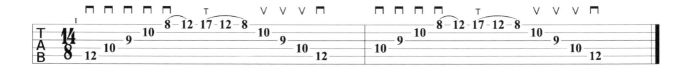

Now with the above lick we are extending the arpeggio by tapping an A. This is the root note. We can also add in a $7^{th}$ or $9^{th}$ or both if we wish to. When I say $7^{th}$ or $9^{th}$, I am referring to the $7^{th}$ and $9^{th}$ notes of the scale. In this case they would be the $7^{th}$ or $9^{th}$ notes of the A minor scale because that is the arpeggio we are playing. (*The $9^{th}$ is the same as a $2^{nd}$*)

*A minor*

| A | **B** | C | D | E | F | G | A | **B** |
|---|---|---|---|---|---|---|---|---|
| 1 | **2** | 3 | 4 | 5 | 6 | 7 | 8 | **9** |

So let's try an extended arpeggio with some tapping where we add in the $7^{th}$ and $9^{th}$ tones of the scale ($15^{th}$ and $19^{th}$ frets on the high E string). This one can be pretty tricky so take your time with it.

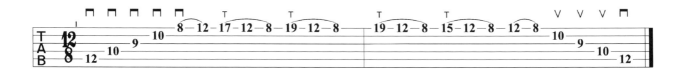

This is a more advanced arpeggio so strive for an even tempo and play it clean!

# Adding Some 3 String Shapes with Tapping

Now let's add a 3 string shape to this tapping arpeggio. Again, these are starting to get rather advanced so be sure that you can execute the 2<sup>nd</sup> inversion minor arpeggio cleanly before attempting this.

## And Now Let's Add the Slide

Let's add the slide technique to the 3 string technique with the tapping technique and see what we get. I'll tell you what we get. We get a very fun, advanced arpeggio to practice. We will again start with the 2<sup>nd</sup> inversion A minor arpeggio but this time we will slide into root position for the finish. Here it is.

Now we are starting to play some pretty difficult arpeggios that utilize different techniques and multiple positions. But let's remember that as difficult as these may seem, all we are doing is playing around with two of the shapes that we should know by now, the root and 2<sup>nd</sup> inversion minor arpeggios.

# A Couple More Advanced Arpeggio Examples

Here are two more examples to demonstrate some of the different techniques we can add to our arpeggios. This first one is in A Harmonic minor and uses a pedal point. This is a very fun and classical sounding way to augment an arpeggio. Pay attention to the picking directions.

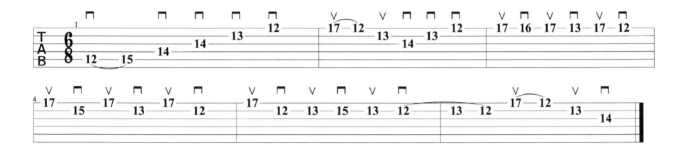

*A Harmonic minor*

This next one is in D minor and utilizes the 2<sup>nd</sup> inversion minor arpeggio while adding a little legato lick at the top of the arpeggio.

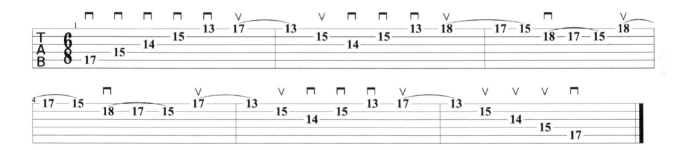

*D minor*

The point is to try and mix in other techniques with your arpeggios so that we aren't just sweeping up and down. We are constructing actual licks that we can use in our playing.

You can see how to use theory and technique to add some spice to your arpeggios. Now let's move on to the next section that covers picking. And if you want to play shred and metal, then this is a technique that you must spend some time with

# SPEED PICKING

Picking is an often overlooked aspect of many guitarists practice routines. Yet it is one of the most important and necessary techniques to master. I remember when I was first trying to seriously improve as a guitarist and I read articles and lessons about "alternate picking". In my somewhat intelligence challenged young brain I thought, "yeah, yeah, yeah, I know how to pick up and down. Now give me something difficult to learn"! Little did I realize at the time that the whole lesson about alternate picking was about *picking very fast and moving to a different string without interrupting the timing of the lick* at all. It was about being able to use the whole fretboard no matter which string I was on!

The most difficult part of playing fast picked runs is when you have to move to a different string. To do this flawlessly is the goal that every good metal / shred guitarist strives for. Picking is something that must be practiced slowly and deliberately. I know I have said this many times but in this instance it is imperative. It is imperative because we do so much of it. I mean we aren't playing arpeggios 95% of the time, we are picking 95% of the time and throwing in an arpeggio every once in a while.

So before we delve too deeply into this great and difficult technique, let's look at a very quick refresher course that demonstrates the difference between the two ways of approaching speed picking, appropriately labeled alternate and economy picking.

# Economy Picking Vs. Alternate Picking

This has been a debate among many guitarists for a while now and I don't believe that there is an answer for which is better. They both have their advantages and disadvantages to be sure. For those of you that don't know the difference between these two methods let me give a very quick tutorial.

I will display the exact same lick but pay close attention to the pick directions. The first is strict alternate picking. Notice how the picking motion is down, up, down, up no matter what.

*Alternate Picking*

Now let's take a look at the other method of picking appropriately named economy picking. Again, pay very close attention to the picking directions as this is what separates the two methods.

*Economy Picking*

Notice how this method sometimes uses two upstrokes or two down strokes in a row. There is no strict up, down, up, down pattern.

# Economy Picking

As you just saw, economy picking sometimes has two or more down strokes in row or two or more upstrokes in a row. The way I prefer to look at this is **THE CLOSEST DISTANCE TO THE NEXT STRING IS A STRAIGHT LINE**. It doesn't matter which direction I have just picked. If the next note is on a higher string I down pick it. If the next note is on a lower string then I use an upstroke.

To me, this makes the most sense. And as you have most likely deduced, this is the way that I learned to pick, although, I also use alternate picking in certain situations when economy picking would be a hindrance. To me, economy picking makes much more sense but I realize that I'm in the minority. Economy picking allows you to do much less work with your pick. It feels a little smoother to execute and is a more efficient technique in my opinion. When I was first starting out, alternate picking made no sense to me. If I am on a down stroke and my next note is on a higher string, alternate picking requires us to skip over the string and come back to pick it with an upstroke.

The difficulties with economy picking are the result of having to change your rhythmic up, down, up picking pattern. You have to learn to actually slow your pick down a little when changing strings. For instance if we were to play three notes on a lower string and then switch to a higher string our pattern would be *down, up, down, down*. Now normally you can play the two down strokes much quicker than alternate picking so you almost have to learn to implement a little slow down motion into your picking. It's not impossible by any means but it does take a little time to learn. Let's take a look at a longer lick.

*E minor*

Notice how the picking pattern employs two down strokes in a row each time we were switching strings when ascending and uses two upstrokes in a row for each string change when descending.

Another interesting fact about economy picking is that it nearly always turns into a predictable pattern. Let's take a look at that same lick but let's start it with an upstroke. Now with alternate picking the whole picking pattern would be the exact opposite as when we started it with a down stroke, but what about the economy picking lick?

*Economy picking when starting with an upstroke*

Notice that the picking pattern *barely* changed at all. The only difference between the two is the first time where we switch to a higher string, the first 3 notes. And that just feels natural because we are employing alternate picking.

One of the major drawbacks of economy picking is that it is a very difficult technique to use if we are doing any kind of "string skipping" lick. Using two up or down strokes in a row and having to cross a string between them is a situation that should be avoided because we always have a tendency to brush against the string in the middle that we did not want to sound. I will demonstrate. Notice how difficult it would be to not hit the B string at all.

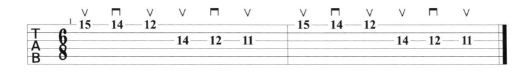

*Very **undesirable** picking pattern*

# Alternate Picking

Alternate picking is the technique of choice for probably 95% of the guitarists in the world. It has been proven many times over to be extremely effective and the majority of the top shredders out there use this technique exclusively. I always felt that you can pick a little quicker with economy picking but I certainly wouldn't say that to Paul Gilbert who is arguably the best alternate picker and string skipper that has ever graced this Earth. So if you need proof that strict alternate picking is an effective technique you don't need to look very far. Let's take a look at that longer lick but employ alternate picking technique.

*E minor*

Now that is about as straight forward as you can get. Down, up, down, up, down, up, forever. So what happens when we start this lick with an up stroke? I almost hate to TAB it out because it is so obvious but just in case I will display it anyways.

So it is the exact same but all of the picking directions are reversed.

# Alternate Picking and String Skipping

Alternate picking lends itself very well to string skipping licks. Remember how difficult it would be to play that string skipping lick that I showed you previously if we had employed economy picking? Let's see how it looks with alternate picking.

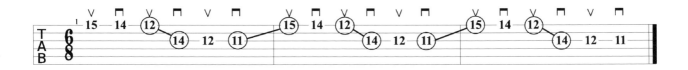

Now this is the optimal picking technique and pattern to play this string skipping lick. We can easily cross over the B string as we are changing our picking direction. If you are going to employ any higher speed string skipping licks that you choose to pick as opposed to legato, this is *THE* way to play it!

One interesting aspect about this though is if we were to start this lick out with a down stroke. With economy picking I stated that this lick would be "very difficult". It's not impossible but I wouldn't want to play it that way if I didn't have to. But with alternate picking, if we start this lick out with a *down stroke* then it is also very difficult to play. So when string skipping, we must think about what picking direction we choose to start the lick out with. I'll demonstrate.

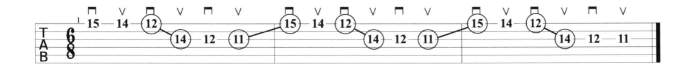

Look at the points where we change strings. I have circled them. See that we have to switch picking direction as we are trying to cross over a string without touching it. This is very undesirable. In this case I would rather just not play the lick at all or I would be sure that I started it out with an upstroke.

# And The Winner Is?

There is no true winner. Try them both and decide for yourself. You will most likely feel drawn to one or the other and it will be an obvious choice for you. To me, economy picking is my weapon of choice for the very fast smooth runs. Alternate picking has a great machine gun like precision to it which is very desirable. There are no rules here, only choices.

When I say that there are no rules, this also implies that there is nothing wrong with using both techniques. They both clearly have their strong and weak points. For fast three note per string runs I almost always will use economy picking. For string skips I always use alternate picking. And, depending on the tone I'm seeking, I will choose the technique that gives me the sound and fluidity that I am looking for.

If you are already solid with your picking technique, be it alternate or economy, I would suggest that you at least dabble in the other technique. You may be surprised at the new licks you can come up with or the fluidity and tone it may add to your playing.

If you are not fully comfortable with your picking yet I suggest that you stick with one technique until you have it close to mastered. Either technique takes time to learn so if you are straddling on the fence and learning both techniques simultaneously you could be adding unnecessary complications to your learning curve. I started with economy picking and then learned how to alternate pick later. Once I had become very comfortable with economy picking learning how to alternate pick came to me at a much faster rate.

# A Few Tips on Practicing Speed Picking

## (Alternate or Economy)

## Try to keep your picking hand locked in place

This is a general "rule" and you, under normal circumstances, do not want to have your fingers that hold the pick moving around. A great way to see this is to just tremolo as fast as you can on a single note. It doesn't matter if it's a fretted note or the open E string. When you perform this tremolo picking *LOOK AT YOUR PICKING HAND*. What position is it? What pick angle do you have? Do your fingers move? Does your wrist move? Your arm? Shoulder? *PAY ATTENTION TO EVERY ASPECT OF YOUR PICKING MOTION WHILE YOU ARE PRACTICING PICKING TECHNIQUE*. We want to keep our picking motions as small and precise as humanly possible. No excess movement if we can help it.

## Strive For Consistency

As I touched upon above, we want to practice with the same hand position, pick angle, style, everything for that matter whether we are tremolo picking or picking a structured lick. Many of us have fallen into this trap. When we are learning to pick and trying to build speed we practice the lick but maybe move our wrist too much. Or change the pick angle. Or any multitude of things. Then, as we start to build speed, we revert back to our tremolo picking positions and style. Why? Don't practice something that you have to unlearn latter. **It takes twice the effort to break a bad habit as it does to just learn it the right way in the first place**. So try to mimic the exact movements that you make when you are tremolo picking. When we are tremolo picking this is our maximum speed and efficiency that we are able to achieve. So do your best to not stray too far from the way that you tremolo pick.

## Use a Metronome

Now I'm not a big metronome guy. Some guitarists use it religiously and they are definitely the better for it. I tend to use it in spurts. But to never use one is not acceptable. You would be doing yourself a great injustice to ignore its benefits because the metronome will point you to your problem areas in less time than it took you to read this paragraph. And the sooner we know our problem areas the sooner we can fix them. You may be surprised when you can play a fast picking lick along with a metronome and you are in perfect time. But, if you *slow* the metronome down a notch or two, you all of a sudden struggle with it. You can play it fast but not slow! Try it. Don't just learn a lick at one tempo only. We want to be able to play our licks at any tempo that the music requires.

## The Most Difficult Part Is Changing Strings

Speed picking is actually rather simple. We often learn how to execute this technique very early in our learning years. The only difficult part of picking is learning how to keep the same rhythmic properties while moving to a different string. If all that we had to learn was how to pick really fast on one string we would all be virtuosos and in no need of practice or outside advice. But alas, there are six (or more) strings on a guitar, and if we want to use them all we must learn how to pick on one string and switch our picking to another in the smoothest, most non-noticeable way that we are capable of. So always remember when working on your picking technique to pay special attention to these transitions. Actually, nearly every practice lick that we employ to work on our picking technique is geared towards helping us improve these transitions, making them smoother and more effortless.

## Always Try To Kill Two Birds with One Stone

When practicing our picking technique we will often have to play many different patterns consisting of multiple fingerings across different strings. So why don't we also use this time to practice our modal theory as well? Why just play random patterns when we could be playing the patterns that we need to know in order to understand modal theory? If we do this, then we have just DOUBLED what we are learning during a practice session. If we practice in this way, what would you tell people if they asked you what you were practicing? Would you tell them "I'm practicing my picking technique"? Would you tell them that "I am practicing modal theory"? In all reality you are practicing both theory and technique simultaneously. *KEEP THIS MINDSET ALWAYS, NO MATTER WHAT YOU ARE PRACTICING, AND YOU WILL REACH YOUR GOALS TWICE AS FAST!!*

## Practice Using Chromatic Scales On Occasion

I have always avoided playing any chromatic scales during practice. My thinking was that I won't use them in my live playing so why should I waste my time using them when I practice. The chromatic scale is not really a scale at all. It is just any note that you decide to play. No theory needed, but you won't be in tune either. So I never really played them at all. I will admit though that as I progressed I started playing around with them a bit. You can design some real finger twister exercises. They can really help develop "finger independence" which is the ability to have complete control over each of your shredding digits regardless of what your remaining fingers are doing. So that being said, spend a little time working with them but don't overdo it.

## Remember To Alter Your Dynamics

One of the great benefits of picking individual notes as opposed to sweeps or legato is that we have so much more control over every single note contained within the lick. We can exploit nearly all of the techniques that we personally use to add flavor to any note of our choice. We can use palm muting, which sounds great on picked runs. We can add vibrato, pinch harmonics, hammer-ons, pull-offs, natural harmonics, slides and trills. We can also easily alter the speed of the lick at any point we choose. We can pick really hard and dig the pick into the strings, back off and use a lighter touch or pick anywhere in between. And perhaps best of all, we can employ the use of bends and vibrato wherever we wish. We can be very expressive when we are picking.

So whenever you are practicing, try to add a little flavor to whatever you are working on. Always experiment with palm muting when you are picking notes. Palm muting sounds really great on the lower notes in a run and then you can back off of it and make the higher notes scream for you.

The bottom line is, don't play like a robot! Add your own little nuances to a lick even when you are just practicing. Let me take that back. Add your own little nuances to a lick *especially* when you are practicing. Practice time is when you learn how to screw around and add squeals, vibrato, bends, slides, and everything else to make those boring scales jump out and define you not only as a guitarist, but as a musician. Practice time is when you can "let it all hang out" and experiment. We aren't worried about trying something that doesn't work because nobody is listening. So experiment during your practice sessions.

# The Essential Alternate Picking Practice Lick

This lick is the most essential practice lick that you can ever perform, particularly when alternate picking is your weapon / technique of choice. This practice lick is labeled by many as "The Paul Gilbert Lick". I am quite certain that he is not the one who "invented" it, but one thing that I am confident about is that he is the one who exploited it and demonstrated the importance of it when learning how to alternate pick. So I hereby give one of the greatest alternate pickers on this planet his just due. Thanks Paul!

*D minor*

This lick should be practiced over and over and over. Play it for a minute or two every time you pick up your instrument. The part we are concentrating on is the upstroke when we change strings. The G fretted 5th fret on the D string. Play this lick in different positions utilizing the scales we have learned. Practice it often. And let's not forget its equally important inverse.

*E minor*

This lick is the inverse of the one above. Concentrate on the string change where you fret the G note on the 10th fret on the A string.

The previous lick is not as important of a learning tool if you choose to employ economy picking. When using alternate picking you are practicing what is known as "outside picking". This term refers to when we are picking two strings in succession and our picking motion is "outside" of the two. When utilizing economy picking the lick teaches us how to employ "inside picking", which means that our pick is staying in-between the two strings. Let me give you a quick example of both.

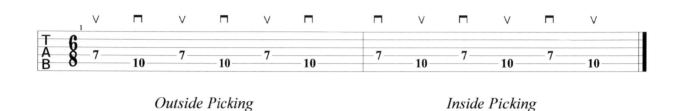

*Outside Picking*                    *Inside Picking*

Eventually you will have to be able to utilize both inside *and* outside picking, no matter which technique you choose. But for now, just know that ***Alternate picking always tends to utilize outside picking*** and ***Economy picking always tends to utilize inside picking***. As I said though, you will have to learn both of them eventually.

So let's take a look at the essential alternate picking lick and its inverse when using economy picking to see just why it will not be as useful of an exercise to develop our economy picking skills.

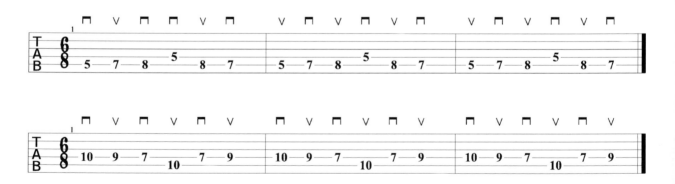

Notice that with economy picking these licks turn into a straight alternate picking after the first measure.

# Economy Picking Essential Lick

This is the last time I will differentiate between economy picking licks and alternate picking licks. All of the remaining lessons will just be "picking licks" and you can decide which method suits you best.

With economy picking, the difficult part to learn is picking two notes in the same direction when changing strings. A great way to overcome this is to just run our three note per string scales up and down. I have always felt that while practicing this way, not only am I practicing economy picking technique, I am also reinforcing modal theory. So let's look at a longer exercise that helps us learn economy picking technique and theory simultaneously.

*A minor*

Notice how this run helps us to practice the two down strokes in a row technique when we ascend followed by reinforcing the two upstroke technique when we descend. With this exercise every time we switch strings we are picking in the same direction as we had just previously picked.

# Picking Practice

This lick is a straight forward up and down scale run that has two string changes incorporated into it. As you build up speed pay close attention to the string changes to be sure that they don't sound any different than the other notes. We should strive for a smooth transition on every string change.

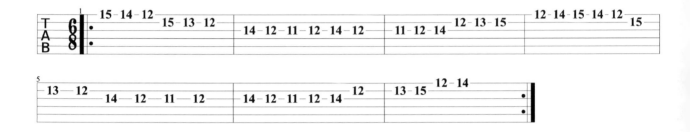

*E minor*

The last exercise was very straight forward so let's try a practice lick that can be used in our soloing and also helps us to practice our string changes and position shifts.

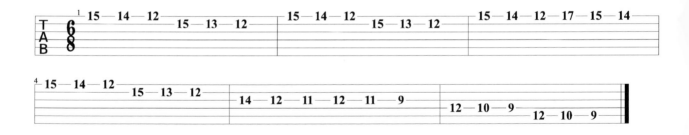

*E minor*

We can really play these at a very quick pace once we get the technique under our fingers. However, always remember to play them cleanly and never practice mistakes.

# More Picking Practice

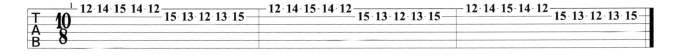

*E minor*

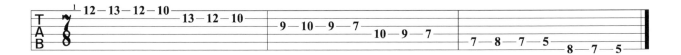

*E minor*

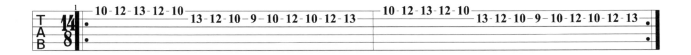

*A minor*

*E Phrygian dominant*

These are just a few examples of some licks and exercises to help us practice our picking technique. I have not included any picking directions. Those are for you to decide depending on whether you are more of an economy or alternate picker.

# Difficult Picking Exercises

Here are a handful of difficult exercises to help us work on our picking. The first exercise seems that it would be easier because it has fewer notes than most but it can prove to be rather challenging. This exercise lends itself well to economy picking. To alternate pick it can be difficult because you are alternating between starting with a down stroke followed by starting with an upstroke. Let's give it a try.

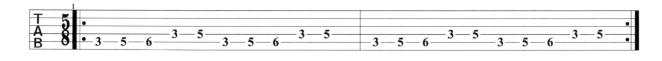

*C minor*

This next lick is very cool sounding and utilizes the A harmonic minor scale. This exercise / lick provides us a great way to practice our outside picking technique. It should be played using alternate picking and the first note should be played with an upstroke. This is a very classical sounding exercise and has been utilized by many neoclassical shredders as well as many famous composers throughout the years.

*A harmonic minor (pedal point)*

Let's take a quick look at a string skipping lick. These can be very difficult to execute cleanly so be sure to take your time and concentrate on the string changes.

*B minor (string skipping)*

# Mixing Legato and Speed Picking

This is a great technique that can help take a little bit of the work from our picking hand. It also gives us the ability to mix two techniques together giving us a nice, unique tonal quality without sacrificing any speed.

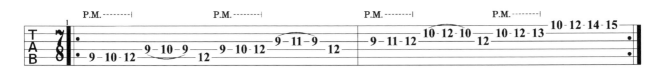

*E minor*

The next lick is similar to the last one and can sound really cool when we add in a little palm muting and vibrato pinch harmonic at the end.

*C minor*

Here is one last lick that mixes the two techniques. This lick has more emphasis on the legato parts.

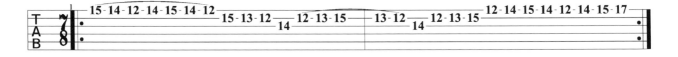

*E minor*

# A Key Shape That We Should Always Be Aware Of

There is a certain shape that, when we find ourselves playing it, always helps us to know where we are. Call it a sort of "Home Base" if you will. When we are playing at high speeds it is always nice to have a symmetrical pattern on adjacent strings. This relieves much of the thinking portion of the lick and allows us to concentrate purely on the technique. Here is a great pattern that we should pay attention to.

Whenever we are in this pattern it is easy to play the upper portion of it and then move back to the lower portion because it is symmetrical. Here is an example in A minor.

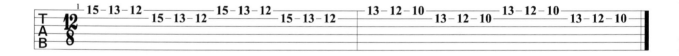

*A minor*

Notice that we only have 2 fingerings to play and they are both symmetrical. This takes much of the thinking portion out of the equation. We can also move this pattern around using octaves to our advantage.

Let's take a look at that same pattern but this time we will extend it using octaves so that we can cover more of the fretboard. Using this method can be an outstanding method to transition from the Aeolian / minor shape on the low end to the Phrygian box on the higher end.

With the above pattern we are able to span an entire 12 frets and use all 6 strings. We accomplished this long span utilizing only one pattern. This is why this particular pattern is a great tool for us to use when we want to transition to a different fretboard area.

Below is an extended run in A minor that takes advantage of this symmetrical pattern. This can be very useful in that it goes from the 15th fret all the way back to the 5th fret.

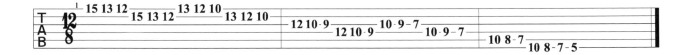

*A minor*

Notice as well that in the above lick we start at the 15th fret and end up at the root position of the A minor scale. So this run took us from the Phrygian box back to our home base of 5th fret A minor scale.

# Building Our Own Practice Exercises

Defining our problem areas and writing little exercises to help us work on those areas is an important part of our continued desire to become better guitarists. We should do this for any technique but here I will focus on some picking exercises.

When it comes to picking all of the notes, one issue in particular can give us headaches. This issue is related to the number of notes that we play on each string. Over time we become quite good at playing three note per string licks because this is a very natural way to divide the scale. However, what if we wanted to play 2 notes, then 3 on the next string, and so on? I will demonstrate.

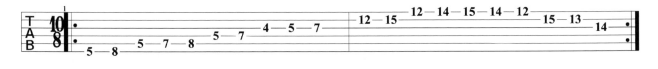

*A minor*

This is actually more difficult to play than it looks. We thought that we were getting pretty good (and we are) at picking, but then all we do is subtract one note from our pattern and we are all out of synch and it feels foreign to play. This is normal. We just have to realize that we need to practice other rhythmic patterns as well.

So what if we wanted to practice playing 4 notes followed by 3 on the next string? We would like to design a practice lick that is repeating so that we can get a lot of bang for our buck. We would also like to design our exercise so that it is diatonic to the scale of our choice

Let's choose D minor as our scale for lack of a better choice. We want to work on playing 4 notes on one string and 3 notes on another. So let's make an exercise.

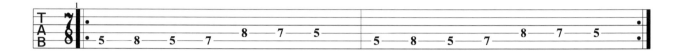

*D minor*

Let's also make sure that we practice the inverse of this exercise as well. We can even change up the notes a bit.

*D minor*

Notice that the exercise that we just designed to help us work on our picking technique has the added benefit of a different fingering, a fingering that we may not be familiar with. Let's try the same picking pattern again but this time we want to work on the higher frets. Let's change the scale to G Phrygian and change the order of the notes as well.

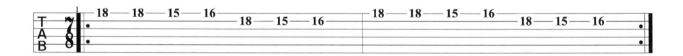

*G Phrygian*

Notice that with this exercise we fret and pick two of the same notes in a row. This needs to be practiced as well. It may seem easy but it has a tendency to throw off our timing.

# What Else Can We Design Into Our Exercises?

When we are designing these exercises we should be sure to work on them in different positions and string sets as well. Many times I like to start in the middle around the 9<sup>th</sup> fret when first designing an exercise. It's a nice, easy position with not too much stretch, yet my fingers aren't too cramped together. But once you are comfortable in that position be sure to practice it on the higher and lower frets as well. Let's try a few more of our 4 and 3 exercises.

This first exercise again has the same picking pattern, but this time we will play it in A major so we can get a bit of stretching practice in for our fretting hand.

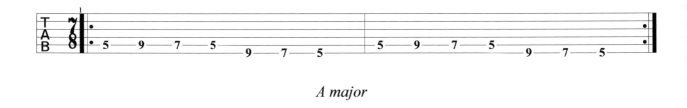

*A major*

Let's also try a cool sounding exercise in A harmonic minor that helps us to work on the higher frets. The higher frets are great to play on but we have to be careful because our precision needs to be addressed as there is not much room for error. Those frets start getting pretty close together once we play past the 12<sup>th</sup> fret.

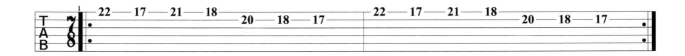

*A harmonic minor*

As you can see, we could go on and on when designing exercises. And we have made all of these from just wanting to work on a 4 note 3 note picking pattern. But we morphed that into fret hand exercises as well. This is a very powerful tool for us to possess!

# Our Two Picking Speed Limits

The way that I see it, we have two speed limits that we must obey when it comes to speed picking. Not surprisingly, these two speed limits are enforced by our own left and right hands and they each have their own maximum speed. Of the two speed limits, unfortunately, we must obey the slower of the two. Let's take a look at the reasons behind these speed limits.

## The Picking Hand

When we tremolo pick a single note this is our top speed for the picking hand. Sure you can work on being able to pick faster but I would imagine that you can already tremolo pick plenty fast. However, if we start adding more strings into the equation then we most likely can work on improving this. If we pick 3 notes on the high E string followed by 3 notes on the B string and keep repeating this pattern then this is our top picking speed for that picking pattern. Let's see an easy exercise.

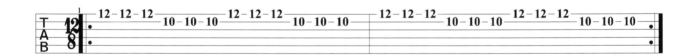

Try and see how fast you can play the above exercise cleanly. If we can only play this at a certain tempo, changing the notes definitely won't help us to add speed. Let's see the exact same picking pattern but with some usable notes and you'll see what I mean.

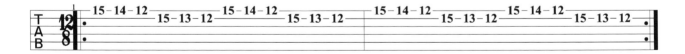

In this instance our picking hand is what slows us down.

# The Fretting Hand

Our other speed limit is our fretting hand. This speed limit is very close to our legato speed. This speed limit basically states that **as fast as we can play the lick legato is the top speed that our fretting hand is capable of** *at this point*. Of course this speed limit is one that we can increase quite a bit with practice. Let's take a look at a simple example.

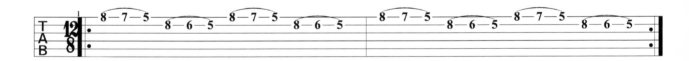

In the above example we are employing legato and our picking hand is doing very little, if any, work at all. We should be able to play this as fast as our fretting hand will allow us. Now if we all of a sudden decide to pick every note, I don't think that our fretting hand will suddenly gain speed, do you? As a matter of fact we may even need to slow our fretting hand down if we find that our picking hand can't quite keep up.

Let's add in another string and see what happens to our speed limit.

*Try to play the above example both legato and picking*. Ideally we want to be able to play them both at the same speed. When we can play either legato or picking at the same speed then this is the point that both our hands have achieved the same speed limit and this is what we should be striving for.

# Back To Our Picking Hand

Just because we can tremolo pick at a certain speed does not mean that we can play at that speed when switching strings. I wish it were that easy. With practice, we begin to become comfortable playing 3 note per string patterns cleanly at some pretty insane speeds. Three note per string scales are built for that. Yet when we start to change up the pattern, all of a sudden our picking hand becomes a huge drag on our speed. Let's look at an example and start out with playing it legato.

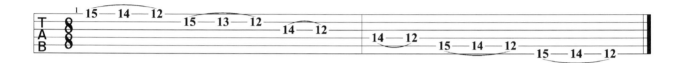

Notice that the lick above is not 3 notes per string any more but we can still play it legato at a pretty fast speed. We weren't slowed down too much.

Let's try the same lick but picking every note.

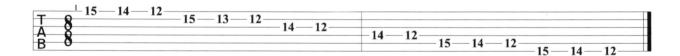

Now we have encountered a major speed bump in our playing. It should be obvious after picking this lick that the picking hand is very often the source of our picking issues. The fretting hand is much easier to get up to speed on most licks while our picking hand is usually very stubborn. Always keep this in mind when learning new licks, especially ones with uneven picking patterns. We normally have to spend twice as much time on our picking hand as we do our fretting hand.

# DEVELOPING OUR OWN STYLE

There are many things that each of us do differently that makes our playing discernible from others; the speed that we bend notes, the speed and "wideness" of our vibrato, the way that we tend to palm mute certain runs or the modes that lean towards when we play. All of these nuances, when summed together, define our individual styles. *And these nuances don't always come to us naturally, contrary to popular thought*. We should work on these parts of our playing just as much as our technique and theory. Let's go over a short list of techniques and ideas that help us to define who we are as musicians.

## VIBRATO

Nothing can separate us more from beginner or intermediate guitarists than having good vibrato technique. This is how guitarists like Eric Clapton, BB King, or Carlos Santana are able to hit one note and make it sing. You can just about tell who the guitarist is with one note. So the chosen pitch of the note is not important, it's the vibrato. I think that when any human being hears that quick, wide, squealing vibrato, they instantly know that Zak Wylde is somewhere within earshot. Some players have a very wide and slower vibrato while others may have a thinner and fast vibrato. And then there are guitarists like ourselves who would love to be able to change our vibrato width and speed as we see fit. To be able to alter the speed and width of our vibrato takes practice. Try hitting one note and using vibrato with a metronome in the background. Try to match the speed of the vibrato to the metronome. It can actually be very fun to do. This is where we can really start to "feel" the music and inject that feeling into our playing, even though we are only playing one note. So make a point to, at least occasionally, practice this technique. PRACTICE YOUR VIBRATO!

# Finger Vibrato

Finger vibrato is most commonly used when we are playing a note but not bending it. This is an easier vibrato to perform but it has its limitations. To employ this technique the lower 3 strings are pulled down while the higher 3 strings are pushed upwards. This technique can afford us great control over the speed and width of the vibrato but is basically unusable if we are in the middle of a bend.

# Wrist Vibrato

This is a more difficult technique to learn and be able to use at will. Wrist vibrato is best used when we bend a note up and vibrato it while holding the bend, although we can also use it most any other time. As the name implies, the vibrato comes from a rocking motion of the wrist and forearm while keeping the fingers locked in place. Use the fretted note and your thumb as a pivot point. As we turn our wrist and forearm at varying degrees the note goes between sharp and flat when in the middle of a bend. This technique, when performed properly, instantly lets everybody know that you know how to play guitar.

Our difficulties lie in numerous areas when learning wrist vibrato during bends. The technique is difficult to learn and the bends must be precise. You should also strive to bend to the target note and then use wrist vibrato to raise the note sharp and then pass back down through the note until it goes flat by the same amount and repeat. This is the big advantage of using wrist vibrato during bends. Finger vibrato allows us to be on the target note and alternate between in tune and sharp. This technique, when coupled with a precise bend, awards us the versatility to hit the target note and then alternate between sharp and flat while hitting the target note in between. So we are in essence "straddling" the target note while we are going above and below it in time and within a certain width of our choice.

## Accurate Bends

Executing a proper bend is imperative to our playing. Little else sounds worse than bending up to a target note and not quite reaching it, or overshooting it for that matter. Bends are easy to practice and should not be ignored. Think about it. You can hear two guitarists play the exact same note, bend it up a whole step, add a little vibrato, and you can instantly know which guitarist is the more accomplished of the two.

Practicing bends is a straight forward exercise. Pick a note. Pick another note either ½, whole, or 1 ½ steps up and bend the 1$^{st}$ note until it perfectly matches the 2$^{nd}$. Make sure to practice this on different strings and different fretboard positions.

And as I mentioned on the previous page, be sure to add some wrist vibrato to your bends once you have reached the target note. A popular technique is to bend up to the target note and hold it there for a split second before adding your vibrato. Many accomplished guitarists use this technique and who am I to argue with success. It sounds killer when executed properly.

## Use Palm Muting

Palm muting sounds great when we are picking fast runs. Also remember that there are different levels of palm muting. We have the ability to go from heavy handed palm muting by really pressing our palm down on the strings with more force, to all levels of lighter palm muting where we can just hear a hint of it in our playing. This technique is not solely reserved for just the lower stings either. This technique can sound really cool when used on the higher strings and higher frets as well.

## Use the Tremolo Bar If You Have One

The tremolo bar has become an instrument all by itself. Many eighties guitarists used it to great extent back in the day and coaxed some very unique sounds from it. Perhaps back then it was overused to some extent as it would seem that many guitarists have gotten away from it nowadays. However, just because it has been done before does not mean that you should never use it. Just use it sparingly in your playing and don't rely on it as a crutch, as did many eighties shredders. Use it to color and enhance your playing, not to define it.

## Use Both Pinch and Natural Harmonics

Who couldn't love the sound of pinch harmonics applied to an overdriven metal guitar tone. These can be squeezed in anywhere we play but they seem to sound particularly good when we use them in the beginning or at the end of a run. Practice using pinch harmonics on the higher strings and frets as well. They are much more difficult to execute there but the payoff when you do hit them right can send shivers down your spine.

## Mix Legato In With Your Speed Picking

I know that I have fallen into this rut in the past. I would either speed pick a run or legato it. I would never mix the two techniques together in the same lick. Looking back, I'm not sure what I was thinking. Why would I not use both? Using both can help take a monotonous sounding lick and add some spice and flavor to it. Not to mention, it can also make the lick easier for us to play.

# Experiment with Different Modes

Using different modes was a large section of this book. Just because you love playing in the Phrygian mode does not mean that you should play that mode exclusively. Having the knowledge of modal theory allows us to play multiple modes and scales that will fit nicely into the rhythms that we play over. You may be surprised at which mode will sound best to your ears, so try a few different ones.

There is also no rule that says once we choose a mode that we have to stay in it. Many great guitarists will start out in one mode then move to another and back again. This can give the effect of having three different guitarists taking turns playing licks. It can give a feeling of surprise and keep the listeners interested while at the same time staying in tune with the background. And remember, the number one thing we want to do is play in tune.

Changing modes can also sound great if the background is in the same key but it changes tempo. Switching to a different mode during this transition can give us some very cool effects. This also helps to separate two different sections of a solo. So experiment with modes and use the knowledge that you have learned. You will be surprised at how many doors it can open for you.

# Phrasing

Phrasing refers to the timing of our playing. When to play fast, when to play slow, when to pause and bend a note all define the way we phrase our licks. Phrasing is such a personal trait among us. Don't fall into the trap of just playing rapid fire licks without taking time to let the music breathe. If there is such a thing as "natural talent" when it comes to guitar, phrasing is it. The mixture of fast and slow, call and answer, is what we are trying to convey to the listener. We aren't trying to show off the cool new $32^{nd}$ note speed lick that we just learned. We are trying to make music. OK, in all reality we do want to show off the $32^{nd}$ note speed lick that we just learned but, we have to make it fit inside the music. If it doesn't fit, throw it out and save it for another song where it does fit. Don't forget that we are playing music. We aren't just showing off new licks. By all means try the desired lick or technique out to see if it fits. But if it doesn't, consider using something else in your arsenal.

# Note Choice

Here when I am using the term "note choice" I am mainly referring to the notes that we end and pause on. Many times at the end of a solo we bend to the desired finish note and add some vibrato for a "grand finale" type finish. This nearly always sounds good and is used often. The predictable part we can get away from is our note choice at the finish.

Experiment with different notes in the scale for the finish. Try a ½ step bend as opposed to a whole step. Sometimes we get in a rut and always bend up to the root note for our finish. There are 7 notes (most likely) in the scale, so try out a few different notes. We know where the notes are now, so let's use them all.

## Now Use What You Have Learned

Now that you have successfully made it through the book be sure to use what you have learned. We can practice picking and arpeggio exercises all day long but if we don't use them in our playing then what was the point? Make a conscience effort to "force" these licks and ideas into your solos. I say "force" because at first it may feel that way. It most likely will not feel natural to add new techniques and patterns into your playing. The only way that I know how to overcome this is to "force" them at first. After a bit of time they will become second nature to you and you will be the better for it. Make yourself put an arpeggio into a certain part of a solo. Make yourself use a speed picking run at certain times. Make yourself use a different mode. You don't have to keep these ideas in your finished product but give them a try.

Experiment with the different modes and you will soon begin to realize their inherent tonal qualities. You will come to know which one to use in order to get that sound that you are looking for.

And now that you are more comfortable with modal theory, there is no rule that says you have to have the backing track first and then write a solo over it. You can write a great solo and then add the chords and background to it afterwards. This way often works well when playing arpeggios over chord changes.

Above all, enjoy your practice sessions. Feel and hear yourself improving. Revel in the fact that whatever you were working on last week has begun to feel smoother and require much less effort a week later. Feel the speed and accuracy increasing everyday that you practice.

## Enjoy That You Are Able To Play Guitar!

# SOME KEY SCALES AND MODES

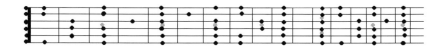

*A Aeolian / minor    (E Phrygian)*

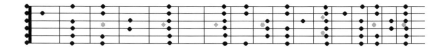

*E Aeolian / minor*

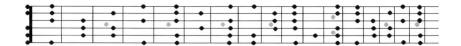

*A Harmonic minor*

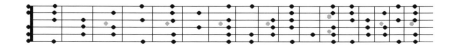

*E Phrygian dominant*

*D Aeolian / minor*

*Diminished (for A Harmonic minor)*

*Move every note up one fret for E Harmonic minor*

# Scales, Modes, and Arpeggios in Chart Form

## The 7 Modes plus Harmonic minor and Phrygian dominant in A

| | | A | A# | B | C | C# | D | D# | E | F | F# | G | G# |
|---|---|---|---|---|---|---|---|---|---|---|---|---|---|
| A | Aeolian | 1 | | 2 | 3 | | 4 | | 5 | 6 | | 7 | |
| A | Locrian | 1 | 2 | | 3 | | 4 | 5 | | 6 | | 7 | |
| A | Ionian | 1 | | 2 | | 3 | 4 | | 5 | | 6 | | 7 |
| A | Dorian | 1 | | 2 | 3 | | 4 | | 5 | | 6 | 7 | |
| A | Phrygian | 1 | 2 | | 3 | | 4 | | 5 | 6 | | 7 | |
| A | Lydian | 1 | | 2 | | 3 | | 4 | 5 | | 6 | | 7 |
| A | Mixolydian | 1 | | 2 | | 3 | 4 | | 5 | | 6 | 7 | |
| A | Harmonic minor | 1 | | 2 | 3 | | 4 | | 5 | 6 | | | 7 |
| A | Phrygian Dominant | 1 | 2 | | | 3 | 4 | | 5 | 6 | | 7 | |

## The A minor Scale and its Modes

| | | A | A# | B | C | C# | D | D# | E | F | F# | G | G# |
|---|---|---|---|---|---|---|---|---|---|---|---|---|---|
| A | Aeolian | 1 | | 2 | 3 | | 4 | | 5 | 6 | | 7 | |
| B | Locrian | 7 | | 1 | 2 | | 3 | | 4 | 5 | | 6 | |
| C | Ionian | 6 | | 7 | 1 | | 2 | | 3 | 4 | | 5 | |
| D | Dorian | 5 | | 6 | 7 | | 1 | | 2 | 3 | | 4 | |
| E | Phrygian | 4 | | 5 | 6 | | 7 | | 1 | 2 | | 3 | |
| F | Lydian | 3 | | 4 | 5 | | 6 | | 7 | 1 | | 2 | |
| G | Mixolydian | 2 | | 3 | 4 | | 5 | | 6 | 7 | | 1 | |

## Arpeggios and Inversions in A

|   | Arpeggio | Inversion |   |   |   |   |   |   |
|---|----------|-----------|---|---|---|---|---|---|
| A | minor | root | A |  | C |  | E |  |
| A | minor | first | C |  | E |  | A |  |
| A | minor | second | E |  | A |  | C |  |
| A | major | root | A |  | C# |  | E |  |
| A | major | first | C# |  | E |  | A |  |
| A | major | second | E |  | A |  | C# |  |
| A | diminished | root | A |  | C |  | Eb |  |
| A | diminished | first | C |  | Eb |  | A |  |
| A | diminished | second | Eb |  | A |  | C |  |
|   |   |   |   |   |   |   |   |   |

## The Aeolian mode / minor Scale in Every Key

|    |       | A | A# | B | C | C# | D | D# | E | F | F# | G | G# |
|----|-------|---|----|---|---|----|---|----|---|---|----|---|----|
| A  | minor | 1 |    | 2 | 3 |    | 4 |    | 5 | 6 |    | 7 |    |
| A# | minor |   | 1  |   | 2 | 3  |   | 4  |   | 5 | 6  |   | 7  |
| B  | minor | 7 |    | 1 |   | 2  | 3 |    | 4 |   | 5  | 6 |    |
| C  | minor |   | 7  |   | 1 |    | 2 | 3  |   | 4 |    | 5 | 6  |
| C# | minor | 6 |    | 7 |   | 1  |   | 2  | 3 |   | 4  |   | 5  |
| D  | minor | 5 | 6  |   | 7 |    | 1 |    | 2 | 3 |    | 4 |    |
| D# | minor |   | 5  | 6 |   | 7  |   | 1  |   | 2 | 3  |   | 4  |
| E  | minor | 4 |    | 5 | 6 |    | 7 |    | 1 |   | 2  | 3 |    |
| F  | minor |   | 4  |   | 5 | 6  |   | 7  |   | 1 |    | 2 | 3  |
| F# | minor | 3 |    | 4 |   | 5  | 6 |    | 7 |   | 1  |   | 2  |
| G  | minor | 2 | 3  |   | 4 |    | 5 | 6  |   | 7 |    | 1 |    |
| G# | minor |   | 2  | 3 |   | 4  |   | 5  | 6 |   | 7  |   | 1  |
| A  | minor | 1 |    | 2 | 3 |    | 4 |    | 5 | 6 |    | 7 |    |

# Harmonic minor Scale in Every Key

| | | A | A# | B | C | C# | D | D# | E | F | F# | G | G# |
|---|---|---|---|---|---|---|---|---|---|---|---|---|---|
| **A** | Harmonic minor | 1 | | 2 | 3 | | 4 | | 5 | 6 | | | 7 |
| **A#** | Harmonic minor | 7 | 1 | | 2 | 3 | | 4 | | 5 | 6 | | |
| **B** | Harmonic minor | | 7 | 1 | | 2 | 3 | | 4 | | 5 | 6 | |
| **C** | Harmonic minor | | | 7 | 1 | | 2 | 3 | | 4 | | 5 | 6 |
| **C#** | Harmonic minor | 6 | | | 7 | 1 | | 2 | 3 | | 4 | | 5 |
| **D** | Harmonic minor | 5 | 6 | | | 7 | 1 | | 2 | 3 | | 4 | |
| **D#** | Harmonic minor | | 5 | 6 | | | 7 | 1 | | 2 | 3 | | 4 |
| **E** | Harmonic minor | 4 | | 5 | 6 | | | 7 | 1 | | 2 | 3 | |
| **F** | Harmonic minor | | 4 | | 5 | 6 | | | 7 | 1 | | 2 | 3 |
| **F#** | Harmonic minor | 3 | | 4 | | 5 | 6 | | | 7 | 1 | | 2 |
| **G** | Harmonic minor | 2 | 3 | | 4 | | 5 | 6 | | | 7 | 1 | |
| **G#** | Harmonic minor | | 2 | 3 | | 4 | | 5 | 6 | | | 7 | 1 |
| **A** | Harmonic minor | 1 | | 2 | 3 | | 4 | | 5 | 6 | | | 7 |

### A Quick Disclaimer about My Method Of Looking At Modes

*Remember when I said that the way I look at and visualize modes is odd because I base them off of the minor scale as opposed to the major scale? There is absolutely nothing wrong with this and I believe it to be more useful in our metal genre. However, the one aspect of it that may give some slight confusion is when scales are "spelled" out. Let's take a look at the C major scale in a different format.*

| All Notes | | C | C# | D | D# | E | F | F# | G | G# | A | A# | B | C |
|---|---|---|---|---|---|---|---|---|---|---|---|---|---|---|
| C Major | | C | | D | | E | F | | G | | A | | B | C |
| Number | | 1 | | 2 | | 3 | 4 | | 5 | | 6 | | 7 | 1 |
| Interval | | | whole | | whole | half | | whole | | whole | | whole | half | |
| C Minor | | C | | D | D# | | F | | G | G# | | A# | | C |
| Number | | 1 | | 2 | 3 | | 4 | | 5 | 6 | | 7 | | 1 |

*The C minor scale contains the notes: C D D# F G G# A#*

*So the "proper" way that the C minor scale (or any minor scale actually) is "spelled" would be to compare it to the major scale.*

### 1, 2, b3, 4, 5, b6, b7

***This is read as 1, 2, flat 3$^{rd}$, 4, 5 flat 6$^{th}$, flat 7$^{th}$***

*Now I'm not sure how much this matters to you. All this means is that if you wanted to tell somebody how to play the minor scale and they already knew the major scale, you are in essence saying that it is the exact same as the major scale but that the 3$^{rd}$, 6$^{th}$ and 7$^{th}$ notes are one fret lower (flatted).*

*Some guitar instructors may scream blasphemy at the way I look at theory but as long as we resolve to the same conclusion, I see no issue with this at all. Either way, just know that anytime a scale is spelled out it is being compared to the major scale.*

*Let's try one more just so we are clear. Let's spell the G dorian mode.*

| G Major | G | | A | | B | C | | D | | E | | F# |
|---|---|---|---|---|---|---|---|---|---|---|---|---|
| G Dorian | G | | A | A# | | C | | D | | E | F | |

| All Notes | G | G# | A | A# | B | C | C# | D | D# | E | F | F# |
|---|---|---|---|---|---|---|---|---|---|---|---|---|
| G Major | G | | A | | B | C | | D | | E | | F# |
| Number | 1 | | 2 | | 3 | 4 | | 5 | | 6 | | 7 |
| G Dorian | G | | A | A# | | C | | D | | E | F | |
| Number | 1 | | 2 | b3 | | 4 | | 5 | | 6 | b7 | |

*So if we wanted to "spell" the dorian mode we would compare it to the major scale. And from the chart above you can see that it is the same as the major scale with the exception of the 3$^{rd}$ and 7$^{th}$ notes, which are flatted. So we would "spell" the dorian mode as:*

**1, 2 b3, 4, 5, 6, b7**

*Read as:* **1, 2, flat 3$^{rd}$, 4, 5, 6, flat 7$^{th}$**

*I suppose this does have its uses at times. The main reason that you should know how this works is so that you can "speak the language". This method was agreed upon a very long time ago and this is often how scales and modes are conveyed to other musicians.*

Made in the USA
Middletown, DE
07 November 2023

42107348R00080